U.S.S. *Tang*
(SS-306)
American Submarine
War Patrol Reports

Also from Riverdale Books

American Submarine War Patrol Report Series

U.S.S. *Cod* **(SS-224)**
ISBN: 1-932606-04-1

U.S.S. *Wahoo* **(SS-238)**
ISBN: 1-932606-01-7

Submarine Fiction

Bacalao
by J.T. McDaniel
ISBN: 0-9172207-5-4

With Honour in Battle
by J.T. McDaniel
ISBN: 0-9712207-3-5

U-859
by Arthur Baudzus
ISBN: 0-9712207-7-8

U.S.S. *Tang* (SS-306)

American Submarine War Patrol Reports

J.T. McDaniel, Editor

Riverdale Books
Riverdale, Georgia

U.S.S. Tang (SS-306): American Submarine War Patrol Reports

This book contains both copyrighted and public domain material. For information , contact the publisher.

Riverdale Books
is an imprint of

Riverdale Electronic Books
P.O. Box 962085
Riverdale, Georgia 30296
www.RiverdaleEbooks.com

ISBN: 1-932606-05-X

Library of Congress Control Number: 2005928385

Printed in the United States of America

Contents

Introduction

The U.S.S. *Tang* (SS-306) is unquestionably one of the most famous American submarines to see service in World War II. In only five war patrols, she set a number of records. In enemy ships sunk during a single patrol, *Tang* placed first and third, sinking 10 ships on her third patrol and seven on her fifth. Her skipper, Commander Richard H. O'Kane, holds the record for most ships sunk by an American submarine commander, with a wartime credit of 31 ships and 227,800 tons. In the category of ships sunk during a single patrol, O'Kane was also on the periscope during the second place patrol, as Executive Officer to Mush Morton in *Wahoo.*

Richard H. O'Kane was born on 2 February 1911, in Durham, New Hampshire. He graduated from the United States Naval Academy with the class of 1934. His initial naval service was in the heavy cruiser U.S.S. *Chester* (CA-27), followed by two years in the old four-stack destroyer U.S.S. *Pruitt.*

He attended Submarine School in 1938, then reported for duty aboard U.S.S. *Argonaut* (SS-166) at Pearl Harbor. Built as a mine-layer, *Argonaut* was the largest submarine in the U.S. fleet at that time, and would hold that distinction until the advent of nuclear power. In addition to her two mine tubes aft, *Argonaut* carried four torpedo tubes forward, and a pair of 6-inch deck guns. O'Kane always evinced a certain fondness for the giant submarine, but was also quite conscious of her shortcomings, which include a limited diving depth, poor maneuverability and, by the time World War II began, a malfunctioning air conditioning system that could no longer control condensation.

On *Argonaut*'s first war patrol, when O'Kane was dive officer, electrical grounds and fires were as much a menace as the enemy. That patrol began rather abruptly, as *Argonaut* was on station near Midway when the Japanese attacked Pearl Harbor. She didn't sink the two Japanese destroyers she encountered, but they didn't sink her, either, which was probably the more likely outcome. *Argonaut* was already scheduled for a major overhaul at Mare Island and probably shouldn't have been anywhere near a combat zone at the time.

Following that patrol, *Argonaut*'s XO was sent to a staff job in Hawaii, and O'Kane was made temporary XO for the voyage back to Mare Island. There he was relieved and sent to U.S.S. *Wahoo* (SS-238) for duty as her first Executive Officer. It was a short journey, as *Wahoo* was being built at Mare Island at that time.

O'Kane was *Wahoo*'s XO during her first five war patrols. The first two, under Marvin Kennedy, were undistinguished. The next three, under the command of Dudley W. "Mush" Morton, were outstanding. Morton devised a system where he would concentrate on the tactical situation while his XO made the periscope and TBT observations and fired the torpedoes. It was a system that worked extremely well in *Wahoo*, but wasn't generally adopted.

When O'Kane was assigned as *Tang*'s first (and only) commanding officer, he went back to the more usual system and did the shooting himself.

As already noted, O'Kane ran up an outstanding record during *Tang*'s five war patrols. He would ultimately receive the Medal of Honor as a result of her last patrol.

Captured after *Tang* was sunk by a circular running torpedo, O'Kane spent the rest of the war in Japanese captivity. He remained in the Navy after the war and retired as a rear admiral in 1957. O'Kane passed away at his home in California in 1994.

The importance of the fleet type submarine in the Pacific Theater during World War II can hardly be overemphasized. While never making up more than 2% of total naval strength, our submarines were responsible for destroying more than half of all Japanese tonnage sunk in the war. So effective were they at sinking Japanese merchant shipping that, during the final months of the war, most found themselves mainly hunting cargo sampans and other small vessels. The big freighters and tanker had, for the most part, already been sunk.

Japanese naval strength was also considerably reduced, partly by sinking, and even more so because our subs had slowed the flow of oil to a trickle by sinking most of the tankers. Several former submariners have suggested that the submarine blockade would have eventually forced the Japanese to surrender without the use of nuclear weapons or the need for invasion.

Our submarines were able to have this tremendous effect on the war in the Pacific despite being handicapped by faulty torpedoes for the first 20 months of the war. Two primary types were available at the beginning of the war. The Mark 10 was an older design, and was used by the S-Boats. While it could be fired from a fleet boat's tubes, gyro and depth setting spindles did not line up, and it was necessary to attach a lanyard to the starting lever to use them. They worked just fine in the S-Boats, of course, which had different tubes. But the Mark 10 was relatively slow (36 knots), and had only a 497 pound warhead. The one thing the Mark 10 did have going for it was that if it hit a target, it would explode.

The standard torpedo for fleet submarines in 1941 was the Mark 14. Also a 21-inch type, the Mark 14's warhead was larger, filled with 660 pounds of TNT at first, and later the same amount of the more powerful Torpex. It was also fitted with what was firmly believed to the ultimate in torpedo technology, the Mark 6 Exploder with it's top secret magnetic influence feature. This was designed to detonate the warhead under the target's keel, insuring fatal damage.

In reality, the magnetic feature never worked properly. It would either detonate as soon as the safety came off (roughly 500 yards into the run), or it wouldn't detonate at all. The contact detonator didn't work very well, either, but that fault was masked by the magnetic feature and the equally unforeseen tendency of the torpedoes to run an average of 11 feet deeper than they were set.

American submarines sank a lot of Japanese ships during the time it took to correct all of these problem, but they probably would have sunk a lot more if the torpedoes had been adequately tested and the bugs worked out before the fighting started. Some have estimated that torpedo problems added as much as a year to the war in the Pacific.

Despite these problems, in the end the submarines became a major factor in the defeat of Japan. What the Germans, with eventually a much larger submarine force, had tried and failed to accomplish in the Atlantic, the United States did accomplish in the Pacific. Japan was effectively blockaded in the home islands.

It took dropping the Atomic Bomb on Hiroshima and Nagasaki to force a final surrender, but the submarines, as much as any other factor, had already defeated Japan.

In preparing these war patrol reports for publication, I have tried to keep the editing to an absolute minimum. Obvious spelling errors have been corrected, and the layout is that of a printed reference book and not a mimeographed report. Here and there I have added, in square brackets, what appears to be an obvious missing word. Square brackets also denote places where the microfiche copies of the reports were unreadable and I was forced to make a best guess as to what was originally typed there. In a few places I have had to admit defeat and simply substitute "[illegible]" for undecipherable text.

J.T. McDaniel, General Editor
American Submarine War Patrol Reports Series
Memorial Day, 2004
Riverdale, Georgia

Background

Richard H. "Dick" O'Kane served in three submarines during World War II, starting the war as dive officer in the huge mine-laying submarine U.S.S. *Argonaut* (SS-166), which was on patrol near Midway at the time of the Japanese attack on Pearl Harbor. Following accepted pre-war doctrine, *Argonaut* made a sound approach on a pair of Japanese destroyers, but was unable to set up an attack.

When *Argonaut* returned to Pearl Harbor, following a first war patrol in large part spent fighting frequent electrical fires and other annoyances, her executive officer was sent to a staff job and O'Kane was temporarily moved into this position. It would be a short tenure, as *Argonaut* was set for an immediate return to Mare Island for new engines and a long list of repairs. Once at Mare Island, O'Kane was assigned as executive officer of U.S.S. *Wahoo* (SS-238), at that time under construction in that yard.

O'Kane served as *Wahoo*'s XO during her first five war patrols. The first two were under Marvin Kennedy, the next three under Dudley "Mush" Morton. With Morton, O'Kane found himself serving as co-approach officer, making the periscope and TBT observations while Morton kept track of the overall tactical situation. It was a technique that worked extremely well for them, and *Wahoo* was credited with sinking 16 ships during the three patrols under the Morton-O'Kane team.

When *Wahoo* returned to Mare Island for overhaul following her fifth war patrol, O'Kane was again detached. This time he was assigned as commanding officer of the under-construction U.S.S. *Tang* (SS-306), a new *Balao* class fleet submarine. *Wahoo*, still under Morton's command, returned to the war and was lost with all hands while exiting the Sea of Japan on her seventh war patrol.

Tang was laid down on 15 January 1943, at the Mare Island Navy Yard, and launched on 17 August. She was placed in commission on 15 October 1943.

The *Balao* class boats were essentially improved *Gato*s. Both types were 311' 9" in length, with a 27' 3" beam. The most obvious external difference was in the conning tower fairwater, which was cut down to an absolute minimum in the *Balao*s.

But the biggest real difference was diving depth. Test depth for a *Gato* was 300 feet. The *Balao*s, built of tougher steel, had a test depth of 400 feet. During her trials, O'Kane established Tang's actual test depth to be 612 feet.

Tang's only commanding officer, O'Kane would become America's leading submarine commander in terms of enemy ships sunk during four of her five war patrols. Her second patrol was mostly spent on lifeguard duty, and no ships were sunk, though *Tang*'s rescue of 22 downed fliers was considered a sufficient trade. O'Kane's total wartime credit (by patrol report endorsement) was 31 ships sunk, and 227,800 tons. Her third war patrol set the record for enemy ships sunk by a submarine during a single patrol, with a total of ten (two more, as it turned out, than O'Kane realized and reported at the time).

Post war, JANAC (Joint Army-Navy Assessment Committee), based on their examination of Japanese records, reduced that credit to 24 ships and 93,824 tons. The JANAC report was never regarded as accurate by wartime submariners, who more than once found that ships clearly seen to sink were disallowed, or other, smaller ships that might have been lost hundreds of miles away credited instead. In 1980, the submarine part of the JANAC report was replaced by the wartime patrol report credits. In Tang's case, the two extra ships from the third patrol stayed on her total, raising it to 33 ships.

Patrol One, 22 January 1944 – 3 March 1944

A16-3   U.S.S. TANG (SS306)
Serial 07   c/o Fleet Post Office
CONFIDENTIAL   San Francisco, California

March 3, 1944

From: The Commanding Officer.
To   :   The Commander in Chief, United States Fleet.
Via   :   The Commander Submarine Division 141.
               The Commander Submarine Squadron 14.
               The Commander Submarine Forces Pacific Fleet.
               The Commander in Chief, U.S. Pacific Fleet.

Subject: U.S.S. *Tang* (SS306), Report of War Patrol # 1.

Enclosures: (A) Subject report.
               (B) Track Charts. (ComSubPac only.)

     1.   Enclosure (A), covering the first war patrol of this vessel conducted in areas north and west of Truk, and north and west of Saipan, during the period 22 January, 1944 to 3 March, 1944, is forwarded herewith.

R.H. O'Kane.

CONFIDENTIAL   **U.S.S. *TANG***

(A) PROLOGUE

After completion December 1, 1943, trained eighteen days in San Diego area. Arrived Pearl January 8, 1944, and continued training through the 19th, having fired forty-three exercise torpedoes and conducted night approaches on approximately half the days underway.

(B) NARRATIVE

Jan 22 - 28:
Left Pearl at noon on the 22nd and proceeded to Wake Island at one engine speed.

Jan 29 - Feb 5 (+12[1]):
Patrolled submerged in vicinity of Wake except during false start for assigned area on the thirty-first. Departed from assigned station to patrol southwest of the island whenever circumstances of special mission permitted, and closed the island daily to insure that no shipping had passed by our seventeen foot periscope or radar searches.

The air strikes on the thirtieth and fifth were carried out without incident. Except for dawn searchlight displays, the only activity observed during the week was ineffectual searching after the first air attack by one or two planes dropping flares sporadically. Observation from within three miles did not disclose any damage to shore installations by the first air attack.

Feb 6 - 7 (-12):
Upon release from lifeguard duty shortly after midnight, proceeded at fifteen knots to newly assigned station north of Truk.

At 1345 on the seventh dived for twenty minutes and avoided an unidentified plane. Slowed to eleven knots at midnight.

Feb 8 (-11):
Sighted U.S.S. *Guardfish* at 1315 and avoided on the surface. Entered assigned area at 1500 and proceeded toward the western boundary to patrol the Truk-Empire routes.

---

1. +12: Indicates the local time zone. In this case, Greenwich Mean Time plus 12 hours.

Feb 9 - 14 (-10):

Patrolling on surface in recommended northwestern part of area, searching with periscope, sound to detect echo ranging, and enjoying unlimited visibility. Converted #3 & 3B to normal ballast tanks.[2]

Feb 14 - 15 (-10):

Patrolled on surface in southwestern part of the area, covering the route from Truk to Saipan which passed north of Namonuito. Proceeded south the night of the fifteenth to patrol east of Mogami and Gray Feather banks prior to assuming new patrol station south of Ulul Island. At 1204 on the fourteenth and at 0925 and 1123 on the fifteenth had plane contact on the SD at 20, 24, and 28 miles. These were tracked out to almost 35 miles.

Feb 16 - 17 (-10):

Conducted submerged patrol east of Mogami and Gray Feather banks with continuous periscope observation, and 17 foot searches. Proceeded toward assigned position twelve miles south of Ulul after sunset.

Attack # 1:

At 0025 on the morning of the seventeenth, sighted a convoy on the SJ, bearing 305T, distance 31,000 yards. It was tracked at eight and one-half knots on base course 100° directly into the rising half moon, and zigging forty degrees every ten to fourteen minutes. As viewed on the radar, excluding side lobes, the convoy was composed of two large ships, a somewhat smaller one, later believed to be a destroyer, a small escort close ahead, two more escorts on either beam, and two more wide flanking patrols.

At 0219, when nearly there, with range to convoy 15,000 yards, the starboard flanking escort suddenly appeared at 7,000 yards closing at four knots. We were forced down and given five depth charges, but his attack was half hearted and we were able to return to radar depth fifteen minutes after he passed by. The convoy was still 9,000 yards away and coming on nicely. Our approach from here in was quite routine, except for additional depth charges and patrolling escorts. Went back to periscope depth at 4,000 yards, watched the leading escort cross conveniently to the opposite bow, the port escort crossing our bow, and at 0335 fired a spread of four straight stern shots at the near

---

2. These ballast tanks were used as fuel-ballast tanks. During the early part of the patrol they are filled with diesel fuel. When the fuel was consumed they were converted back to normal ballast tanks. Conversion involved opening the Kingston (flood) valves and reconnecting the vent linkage, then flushing out any residual oil.

AK[3], range 1,500, 80 port track, speed 8½. The first three hit their points of aim in the screws, and the after and forward ends of the midships superstructure. Watched the freighter sinking by the stern amidst milling escorts. She was a split superstructure freighter, with details similar to the *Mansei Maru*, low in the water, with a bulky deck load.

When she had sunk we went to our favorite depth below the 375 foot gradient and cleared the area. Some additional depth charging followed, but none close, and we were able to search with radar and surface at 0500.

Feb 16 - 17 (-10):

There were still ships in sight on the radar with one large escorted one at 14,000 yards, which we tracked on course 300, speed seven knots. During the next forty minutes we pushed our TVG's and MEP's[4] in charging and getting ahead of the freighter, but he evidently had been on a northerly leg of a wandering zig, for during the submerged approach in the next six hours he presented angles of 50 starboard to 150 port. Our best sustained speed closed the range to 6,000 yards at one time, but he then drew slowly away and disappeared toward the *Burrfish* who evidently made contact with him. The *Asashio* destroyer, a *Chidori*, a PC type escort, and a plane which were escorting him precluded an end-around, so proceeded submerged to our assigned position for the attack on Truk. The freighter, in ballast, was a typical goalpost, funnel, goalposter with composite superstructure.

Feb 18 - 19 (-10):

Patrolling on the surface in the vicinity of assigned position 12 miles bearing 194° from Ulul. As our SJ gave fair contact on this 85 foot island at 33,000 yards, remained about four miles south of assigned position out of sight of the island. Numerous SD contacts, only one of which was closer than the range to the island, and most of which disappeared at the distance to the island, indicated considerable patrol or plane escort activity from Ulul. We dove for a half hour and apparently avoided detection by the one plane that did close our station inside fifteen miles.

Feb 20 - 21 (-10):

Shortly after dawn on the twentieth proceeded toward new station at Saipan, running at one engine speed. During the forenoon numerous SD contacts from

---

3. AK: Freighter.
4. TVG and MEP: Temperature-Voltage-Gravity curve and Maximum Effective Pressure. The first is a measure of battery charging rate. Exceeding the curve can result in excess hydrogen gas generation. The second is a measure of engine loading.

20 to 28 miles indicated air activity and perhaps a plane escort for a convoy. Searches ten miles either side of our track revealed nothing.

At 0930 the morning of the twenty-first, a half hour after our trim dive, commenced submerging for enemy patrol planes. We thought we were undetected by the first one, sighted at twelve miles, but four dives later in as many hours, with lookouts reporting planes in different sectors and SD contacts closing, dived for the rest of the day.

Feb 22 (-10):

Patrolled submerged ten miles southwest of Aguijan Island, where we would be able to intercept traffic from Saipan to Guam passing north or south of Tinian. Sighted one surface patrol on the SJ on approaching this spot and avoided submerged after daylight. Bombers continuously passed close over us during the day. At dusk we surfaced to observe considerable searchlight signaling in the vicinity of Tanapag harbor, so headed north at two engine speed to intercept any escaping ships. Our usual SJ performance was cut down by surrounding rain squalls, barely indicating the island at 35 miles, but at 2200 the SJ sighted our first ship at 14,000 yards. Closed and tracked and soon had five ships in sight on the radar, with another group sometimes visible to the north. The persistant rain squalls were both for and against us at this time, for they changed the relative size of the pips and made visual investigation of the enemy inside 3,500 yards essential in selecting suitable targets.

Attack # 2:

Following two such approaches on patrols, we found a *Kenyo Maru* type AK with escorts on starboard bow and quarter. After tracking this freighter zigging on course 255T for another half hour, moved into position on his port bow, 4,000 yards from his nearest escort. An unpredicted zig required a "dipsy doodle" to maintain an ideal firing position, but he came on nicely, and at 2349, with range 1,500, 90 port track, and *Tang* dead in the water and holding our breath, let him have four torpedoes spread his length from aft forward by constant TBT[5] bearings. The enemy literally disintegrated under four hits and sank before we had completed ninety degrees of our turn to evade. One escort guessed

---

5. TBT: Target Bearing Transmitter. A pair of pressure proof binoculars with an illuminated reticule, mounted on a pelorus. A mechanism in the base transmits the bearing to the conning tower when a button on one of the handgrips is pressed. There were two of these on a fleet submarine, one mounted on the forward bridge bulwark, and another on a tripod abaft the periscopes for taking bearings astern. Used during surface attacks.

right and closed to 3,000 yards, but these boats always seem to find a couple of extra knots for such occasions, and we made a sandblower out of him.

Feb 23 (-10):
Attack # 3:

We still had difficulty in identifying the enemy on the radar, and our next approach, in spite of sound, developed into a destroyer at 3,500 yards, with *Tang* backing down 1,200 yards off her track. Both sea and visibility precluded anything but a defensive attack on such a ship, so pulled clear with minimum range 2,900 yards. There followed one more approach, a bit more cautious, on what appeared to be a submarine, before we located what was apparently a naval auxiliary, definitely of the *Arimasan Maru* class. As her leading escort conveniently moved out to 8,000 yards ahead, we moved into position on her port bow, stopped, and kept pointed at her with another nice rain squall for a background. As she came on her guns were plainly visible forward and then aft. At 0120, with range 1,400, 90 port track and gyros around zero, let her have four torpedos spread her length from aft forward. The first two were beautiful hits in her stern and just aft of the stack, but the detonation as the third torpedo hit forward of his bridge was terrific. The enemy ship was twisted, lifted from the water as you would flip a spoon on end, and then commenced belching flame as she sank. The *Tang* was shaken far worse than any depth charge we could remember, but a quick check, as soon as our jaws came off our chests, showed no damage except that the outer door gasket of number five tube, which was just being secured, blew out of its groove. We considered this lightly at the time.

As is usually the case when you hit first, the escorts were befuddled and evasion was simplified. It is considered that this ship was either a submarine or destroyer tender, or an ammunition ship.

Further searches and one more approach disclosed only three patrol type vessels, so commenced a retiring search, covering possible positions of the northern enemy group. An all day search on the surface to north and then retiring to the west disclosed nothing.

Feb 24 (-10):

Patrolled on the surface, 150 miles west of Saipan, searching with high periscope and radar when horizon was fuzzy. At 1109 sighted smoke bearing 015T and immediately picked up two targets on the SJ at 23,000 and 24,000 yards. With a clearing horizon the enemy was shortly identified as a freighter, large tanker, and destroyer. Tracking showed them on course 270, so we moved out to maximum radar range to avoid detection and gained position ahead for a submerged approach. Contact was suddenly lost, but a half hour run at full power toward their last true bearing located them again, this time on base course 165T.

Gathering rain squalls made it more apparent that we would do well to maintain contact with the enemy during the remainder of the day, and that the only possibility of destroying both ships lay in night, or night and dawn attacks. The remainder of the day became more trying with the enemy employing wide zigs and all contact being lost in extremely heavy passing squalls. Sometimes he would emerge on a new course, sometimes on the same, but in most cases it was necessary for us to go in after him at full power, and then retire to avoid detection.

Attack # 4

At sunset the destroyer came into a clear spot, sent several signals on a large searchlight to his convoy, lined them up with tanker astern, and started off on course west. As soon as they had faded in the dusk we closed from east toward Saipan. The enemy zigs were of the wildest sort, sometimes actually backtracking, but their very wildness was his undoing, for after two hours of tracking, and two more of approaches on their quarters, with our outer doors open for firing on four different occasions, the freighter, a *Tatutaki Maru* class ship, made one of his super right zigs across our bow. At 2230, when the range was 1,400, 95 starboard track, gyros around zero, we cold-cocked him with the first three of our usual four torpedoes, spread along his length by constant TBT bearings. The ship went to pieces, and amidst beautiful fireworks sank before we had completed our turn to evade. The tanker opened fire fore and aft immediately, while the destroyer, then nearly 3,000 yards away, closed the scene rapidly, spraying shells in every direction. After helping out any possible survivors with twelve depth charges, she rejoined the tanker. During the first flurry some tracer shells came within a thousand yards or so of us, but obviously just by chance.

The destroyer now stayed so close to the tanker that for several hours we could distinguish only one ship on the radar most of the time, from our position ten thousand yards on his port beam. The sporadic gun firing and occasional depth charges convinced us on these occasions that both were still there. They continued on the same base course, but settled down to moderate zigs. Before dawn we were in position, ten thousand yards ahead and still eighty miles west of Saipan. Only a daylight change of base course could prevent our attack.

Attack # 5

At 0548, with skies gray in the east, submerged to radar depth, took a last check at range 7,000 yards, then started a submerged approach to close an apparent 30° left zig. Eighteen minutes later the tanker was in sight with an *Asashio* type destroyer patrolling very close ahead. As we were then 1,200 yards from the track, turned and paralleled his base course. At range 2,000 yards the destroyer gave us some bad moments by crossing to our bow for the second time, pointed directly at our position. But in his attempt to prevent a repetition of his mistake of the night before, he turned right, passed down the tanker's starboard side to that quarter. He was absolutely dwarfed by the length of the loaded tanker, whose details were now plainly visible. She was painted slate gray, comparable only to our *Cimarron*[6] class, but with bridge and foremast well forward, just behind a bulging bow, which mounted an estimated six inch gun. Her mainmast was close against her after superstructure which was topped by an extremely large short stack. Her after gun, above her bulging cruiser stern, was similar to the one forward. There is no similar vessel in any of the identification books aboard. All vantage points including guns, bridge, bridge overhead, and rails, were manned with an estimated 150 uniformed lookouts on our side alone.

A twenty degree zig toward put us a little close to the track, but as we had already commenced our turn away for a stern shot, we were far from inconvenienced. At 0639, with the escort just crossing the tanker's stern to the far side, fired four torpedoes by constant bearings, range 500 yards, 90 starboard track, gyros around 180°. The first three hit as aimed, directly under the stack, at the forward end of his after superstructure, and under his bridge. The explosions were wonderful, throwing Japs and other debris above the belching smoke. He sank by the stern in four minutes, and then we went deep and avoided. The depth charges started a minute later, but were never close.

Our blown torpedo tube gasket, which we considered lightly on the 23rd, now caused trouble, for the inner door gasket rolled out of its groove under the pressure, and pumps would not keep up with the water. With safety tank nearly dry, regained good control at 80 feet and avoided for the rest of the day at this depth, with occasional looks at 60 feet when our destroyer came close. He was persistent, probably hearing our pumps, one of which had to be run continuously, and spurred on, too, by thoughts of a slit belly if he failed. Dark finally came after our longest day, and a new inner door gasket was installed without much trouble after surfacing. T-shaped gaskets, similar to those just installed in hatches, should obviously by installed in inaccessible torpedo tube outer doors at the first practicable date.

---

6. U.S.S. *Cimarron* (AO-22), displacement 7,470 tons, length 553', beam 45', draft 32' 4". Commissioned in 1939, this large oiler remained in service until 1968.

With four forward torpedoes left, proceeded northward toward the lower Bonins, our new patrol area.

Feb 26 (-10):
Attack # 6:

Patrolled on the surface, proceeding to new area. At 1545, when about 180 miles northwest of Saipan, sighted smoke which quickly developed into a four ship convoy. Tracked them on course 160 until dark, identifying one as a two-stacker. Remained outside 10,000 yards until moonset, when radar tracking showed them to be worm turning[7], on base course east. The rear ship of the convoy was small with a patrolling escort astern that we could not see at 3,000 yards, so passed him up in searching for our two stacker. We found her shortly, astern of the leading freighter, and just ahead of a small unidentified vessel.

Escorts on either bow of the leading freighter offered no difficulty in closing the two stacker from the flank. She was now tracked on straight course 090 and we watched her closely from 3,000 yards before closing in to a firing position. A column zig brought the leading freighter across our port bow, so twisted left, steadied, and fired our usual spread of four torpedoes covering the entire length of the two stacker as he came by, radar range 1,600, gyros near zero, 100 starboard track. All torpedoes, even the the one fired at his bow, apparently missed astern, as we failed to detect his increasing speed as he resumed worm turning. Had a little difficulty in evading the escorts as one closed after we thought we were clear. He challenged us with "S8" on a signal searchlight several times, which furthers our suspicion that the lagging escort, which we could not see at 3,000 yards, was an enemy submarine.

Though it was disappointing not to destroy this passenger ship, the *Horai Maru*, there is no use in crying over spilt milk. The Tang is far from cocky, and just as determined as ever.

Sent contact report on 450, and message to ComSubPac concerning expenditure of torpedoes, then headed for Midway on route prescribed for another of our submarines.

February 27 – March 3

Enroute Midway.

---

7. Worm turning: A type of double zigzag course in which the base course takes on the shape of a large sine wave with smaller zigs moving back and forth across that curving base course.

(C) WEATHER

Normal for all localities patrolled.

(D) TIDAL INFORMATION

Normal for all localities patrolled

(E) NAVIGATIONAL AIDS

None sighted.

(F) SHIP CONTACTS

No.	Time	Date	Lat	Long	Types	Range	Course	Speed	How Cont.
1	0023	2/17	8-10 N	149-07 E	2 AK, 1 DD, 5 Escort	30,000	082	8.5	R
2	0600	2/22	Saipan	Channel	2 Patrol Boats	15,000	Various		R
3	2200	2/22	15-4 N	145-12 E	3 AK, 1 DD, 3 Escort	14,000	270	9	R
4	1109	2/24	15-30 N	143-00 E	1 AK, 1 AO, 1 DD	23,000	165	9	SD
5	1545	2/26	18-10 N	143-00 E	1 AP, 2 AK, 4 Escort	25,000	160, 090	9	SD

(G) PLANE CONTACTS

No.	Time	Date	Lat	Long	Types	Range	Course	Speed	How Cont
1	1346	2/7	14-50 N	159-10 E	Float Plane	6			SD
2	1204	2/14	10-25 N	150-23 E		24	310		R
3	0629	2/16	7-47 N	149-08 E		8			SD
4	1050	2/19	8-30 N	149-50 E		5			SD
5	1435	2/20	9-18 N	149-02 E		7			SD
6	0925	2/21	12-26 N	147-06 E	Flying Boat	17	320		SD
7	1003	2/21	12-29 N	147-05 E	Flying Boat	15	240		SD & R
8	1050	2/21	12-30 N	147-05 E		9			R
9	1309	2/21	12-38 N	147-00 E		16-6			SD & R
10	**	2/22	14-44 N	145-25 E	Many two engine Bombers	Var	Var		Per
11	0830	2/27	19-10 N	145-25 E		10	180		SD & R

** Planes were sighted taking off or landing on Tinian at almost every periscope observation.

U.S.S. Tang (SS306)   Torpedo attack No. 1   Patrol No. 1
Time 0335   Date: 17 February, 1944   Lat 8-04 N.
                                                      Long 149-28 E

TARGET DATA – DAMAGE INFLICTED

Description of target: Two medium AK's, one destroyer, five small escorts.
                          Contact by radar, visibility excellent with three quar-
                          ter moon.
Ships sunk: One AK (*Hansei Maru* class) 7,770 Gross tons.
Ships Damaged: None
Damage determined by: Saw three torpedoes hit and observed ship sink.

Target data: Draft 25 feet, Course 082, Speed 8.5, Range 1,500
Own data: Speed: 3, Course 000, Depth 60', Angle 1° down

FIRE CONTROL AND TORPEDO DATA #1

Type attack	Night radar & periscope.			
Tubes fired	#7	#8	#9	#10
Track angle	75P	79P	81P	83P
Gyro angle	187	183	181	179
Depth Set	6'	6'	6'	6'
Power	High	High	High	High
Hit or miss	Hit	Hit	Hit	Hit
Erratic	No	No	No	No
Mk torpedo	14-3A	14-3A	14-3A	14-3A
Serial no.	40097	39183	39327	39812
Mk exploder	6-1A	6-1A	6-1A	6-1A
Serial no.	446	8273	6358	8441
Actuation	Contact	Contact	Contact	Contact
Mk warhead	16	16	16	16
Serial no.	1162	363	10953	1899
Explosive	TPX	TPX	TPX	TPX
Firing interval	8 sec.	8 sec.	10 sec.	
Type spread	Divergent point of aim			
Sea condtions	Calm			
Overhaul activity:	U.S.S. *Bushnell*			

U.S.S. Tang (SS306)   Torpedo attack No. 2   Patrol No. 1
Time 2349 (-10)   Date: 22 February, 1944 Lat 14-47 N.
                                                Long 144-50 E.

TARGET DATA – DAMAGE INFLICTED

Description of target: Three merchantmen, one DD, at least three small escorts. Contact by radar, visibility poor.
Ships sunk: One AK (*Kenyo Maru* class) 6,486 gross tons.
Ships Damaged: None
Damage determined by: Four torpedo hits seen, ship observed to sink immediately.

Target data: Draft 26 feet, Course 270, Speed 9, Range 1,500
Own data: Speed: 0, Course 000, Depth Surf, Angle 0

FIRE CONTROL AND TORPEDO DATA #2

Type attack	Night surface.			
Tubes fired	#3	#4	#5	#6
Track angle	94P	96P	98P	100P
Gyro angle	357	355	353	351
Depth Set	10'	10'	10'	10'
Power	High	High	High	High
Hit or miss	Hit	Hit	Hit	Hit
Erratic	No	No	No	No
Mk torpedo	14-3A	14-3A	14-3A	14-3A
Serial no.	40194	40109	20068	24905
Mk exploder	6-1A	6-1A	6-1A	6-1A
Serial no.	8379	12375	8655	8284
Actuation	Contact	Contact	Contact	Contact
Mk warhead	16	16	16	16
Serial no.	10969	1747	10902	1870
Explosive	TPX	TPX	TPX	TPX
Firing interval	8 sec.	8 sec.	8 sec.	
Type spread	Divergent point of aim			
Sea condtions	Choppy			
Overhaul activity:	U.S.S. *Bushnell*			

U.S.S. Tang (SS306)	Torpedo attack No. 3	Patrol No. 1
Time 0120	Date: 23 February, 1944	Lat 14-45 N.
		Long 144-32 E.

TARGET DATA – DAMAGE INFLICTED

Description of target:	Same as attack #2.
Ships sunk:	One Naval Auxiliary; Ammunition ship (AK), Destroyer tender (AD), or Submarine tender (AS) (*Arimasan Maru* class) 8,663 gross tons or 10,462 DW tons.
Ships Damaged:	None
Damage determined by:	Three torpedoes seen to hit. Target exploded and sank immediately.

Target data: Draft 28 feet, Course 270, Speed 8, Range 1,400
Own data: Speed: 0, Course 340, Depth Surf, Angle 0

FIRE CONTROL AND TORPEDO DATA #3

Type attack	Night surface.			
Tubes fired	#3	#4	#5	#6
Track angle	102P	104P	105P	106P
Gyro angle	009	007	006	005
Depth Set	10'	10'	10'	10'
Power	High	High	High	High
Hit or miss	Hit	Hit	Hit	Miss
Erratic	No	No	No	No
Mk torpedo	14-3A	14-3A	14-3A	14-3A
Serial no.	23020	40085	22309	40121
Mk exploder	6-1A	6-1A	6-1A	6-1A
Serial no.	7345	7340	9662	8456
Actuation	Contact	Contact	Contact	Contact
Mk warhead	16	16	16	16
Serial no.	10928	11072	10254	311
Explosive	TPX	TPX	TPX	TPX
Firing interval	8 sec.	8 sec.	8 sec.	
Type spread	Divergent point of aim			
Sea condtions	Choppy			
Overhaul activity:	U.S.S. *Bushnell*			

U.S.S. Tang (SS306)   Torpedo attack No. 4   Patrol No. 1
Time 2230   Date: 24 February, 1944   Lat 15-16 N.
    Long 143-12 E.

TARGET DATA – DAMAGE INFLICTED

Description of target: One AK, One AO, One DD. Contact by sight in daylight. Attack at night, visibility poor.
Ships sunk: One AK (*Tatutaki Maru* class) 7,064 gross tons.
Ships Damaged: None
Damage determined by: Saw three torpedoes hit and ship sink.

Target data: Draft 27 feet, Course 115, Speed 8, Range 1,400
Own data: Speed: 5, Course 085, Depth Surf, Angle 0

FIRE CONTROL AND TORPEDO DATA #4

Type attack	Night surface.			
Tubes fired	#2	#3	#4	#6
Track angle	104S	105S	106S	107S
Gyro angle	355	356	357	358
Depth Set	10'	10'	10'	10'
Power	High	High	High	High
Hit or miss	Hit	Hit	Hit	Miss
Erratic	No	No	No	No
Mk torpedo	14-3A	14-3A	14-3A	14-3A
Serial no.	22294	40083	39830	40137
Mk exploder	6-1A	6-1A	6-1A	6-1A
Serial no.	7754	12709	8442	7774
Actuation	Contact	Contact	Contact	Contact
Mk warhead	16	16	16	16
Serial no.	11488	10924	11558	2698
Explosive	TPX	TPX	TPX	TPX
Firing interval	8 sec.	8 sec.	8 sec.	
Type spread	Divergent point of aim			
Sea condtions	Choppy			
Overhaul activity:	U.S.S. *Bushnell*			

U.S.S. Tang (SS306)	Torpedo attack No. 5	Patrol No. 1
Time 0639	Date: 25 February, 1944	Lat 15-50 N.
		Long 144-21 E.

TARGET DATA – DAMAGE INFLICTED

Description of target: Same as #4.
Ships sunk: One Naval Tanker (Comparable to U.S.S. *Cimarron*)
                        18,276 DW tons.
Ships Damaged: None
Damage determined by: Saw three torpedo hits, observed ship sink.

Target data: Draft 30 feet, Course 145, Speed 10, Range 500.
Own data: Speed: 3, Course 233, Depth 60', Angle 0.

FIRE CONTROL AND TORPEDO DATA #5

Type attack	Dawn submerged.			
Tubes fired	#1	#2	#3	#6
Track angle	80S	83S	88S	93S
Gyro angle	172	175	180	185
Depth Set	10'	10'	10'	10'
Power	High	High	High	High
Hit or miss	Hit	Hit	Hit	Miss
Erratic	No	No	No	No
Mk torpedo	14-3A	14-3A	14-3A	14-3A
Serial no.	24675	22233	26020	39799
Mk exploder	6-1A	6-1A	6-1A	6-1A
Serial no.	18214	8389	8452	8439
Actuation	Contact	Contact	Contact	Contact
Mk warhead	16	16	16	16
Serial no.	2671	10996	10939	1150
Explosive	TPX	TPX	TPX	TPX
Firing interval	8 sec.	8 sec.	8 sec.	
Type spread	Divergent point of aim			
Sea condtions	Choppy			
Overhaul activity:	U.S.S. *Bushnell*			

U.S.S. Tang (SS306)   Torpedo attack No. 6   Patrol No. 1
Time 2241   Date: 26 February, 1944   Lat 17-48 N.
    Long 143-40 E.

TARGET DATA – DAMAGE INFLICTED

Description of target: One AP, Two AK's, Four escorts.
Ships sunk: None
Ships Damaged: None
Damage determined by:

Target data: Draft 24 feet, Course 100, Speed 8.5, Range 1,700.
Own data: Speed: 8, Course 028, Depth Surf., Angle 0.

FIRE CONTROL AND TORPEDO DATA #6

Type attack	Night surface.			
Tubes fired	#1	#2	#3	#6
Track angle	100S	102S	104S	107S
Gyro angle	353	355	357	000
Depth Set	10'	10'	10'	10'
Power	High	High	High	High
Hit or miss	Miss	Miss	Miss	Miss
Erratic	No	No	No	No
Mk torpedo	14-3A	14-3A	14-3A	14-3A
Serial no.	40162	40105	23830	39928
Mk exploder	6-1A	6-1A	6-1A	6-1A
Serial no.	8032	11049	6557	8377
Actuation	Contact	Contact	Contact	Contact
Mk warhead	16	16	16	16
Serial no.	11438	2100	11351	3902
Explosive	TPX	TPX	TPX	TPX
Firing interval	8 sec.	8 sec.	10 sec.	
Type spread	Divergent point of aim			
Sea condtions	Choppy			
Overhaul activity:	U.S.S. *Bushnell*			

(I) MINES AND MINE LAYING

None observed.

(J) ANTI-SUBMARINE MEASURES AND EVASION TACTICS

Numerous escorts were encountered with every contact, but their patrolling was unsystematic and sooner or later left an opening for attack, generally on the flank. As it was possible to come up unbelievably close on the quarter of an escort without being sighted, poor stern or quarter lookouts on their part is indicated.

Their gunfire and depth charging was of the wildest sort and most ineffectual. As always, evasion was easy when the enemy was hit first, and much simplified by the PPI.

(K) MAJOR DEFECTS

None.

The only design weakness encountered is the old type dove-tail gasket in torpedo tube doors. Replacement of the outer door gasket is impossible, except in the calmest sea, and its failure immediately limits a submarine to dangerously shallow depths. As hatch gaskets, which are readily accessible are now of the T type, it seems evident that torpedo tube door gaskets should be modified likewise as soon as practicable.

(L) RADIO

Both receptions and transmission were satisfactory.

(M) RADAR

Although requiring considerable checking and attention by radar personnel, both SJ and SD worked reliably and were of great value.

(N) SOUND GEAR AND SOUND CONDITIONS

Good.

(O) DENSITY LAYERS

1. 8-10 N   149-20 E   6° at 375
2. 15-45 N   144-22 E   5° at 475

(P) HEALTH AND HABITABILITY

Good.

(Q) PERSONNEL

Although training in diving was limited by the requirements of the patrol areas, this was in large part compensated for by the extra efforts to qualify that always accompany surface patrolling.

(R) MILES STEAMED – FUEL USED

(a) Pearl to first area	4,272 mi.	29,100 gals.
(b) In areas	2,310 mi.	23,400 gals.
(c) Last area to Midway	2,300 mi.	27,330 gals.

(S) DURATION

Days enroute to areas:		13
Days in areas:	Wake	7
	North of Truk	6
	West of Truk	4
	West of Saipan	5
Days enroute from area:		6
Days submerged (Including 6 days off Wake):		10

(T) FACTORS OF ENDURANCE REMAINING

Torpedoes	Fuel	Provisions	Personnel
None	20,000	40 days	Indefinite

Limiting factor this patrol – Torpedoes.

(U) REMARKS

None.

Submarine Division Sixty-One

F35-61/A16-3

Care of Fleet Post Office,
San Francisco, California,
March 4, 1944

CONFIDENTIAL

First Endorsement to
U.S.S. *Tang* Report of
First War Patrol.

From: The Commander Submarine Division Sixty-One.
To: The Commander-in-Chief, United States Fleet.
[Via:]   (1) The Commander Submarine Force, Pacific Fleet,
                Subordinate Command.
            (2) The Commander Submarine Force, Pacific Fleet.
            (3) The Commander-in-Chief, U.S. Pacific Fleet

Subject: U.S.S. *Tang* – Report of First War Patrol.

1.   This was the first war patrol for the *Tang* and the first of Lieutenant Commander R.H. O'Kane as a Commanding Officer. The patrol was of forty-one days duration, of which twenty-two were spent in assigned areas and nineteen days enroute. Patrol was terminated when all torpedoes had been expended.

2.   The early part of the patrol consisted of lifeguard duty for downed planes in the vicinity of Wake and Truk. The *Tang* was apparently not called on for [*sic*] rescue survivors. Area coverage was thorough. During patrol four contacts were made with groups of ships including targets worthy of torpedo attack. Attacks were made on each group.

3.   (A) Early morning 17 February a convoy of two freighters with a heavy escort of a destroyer and five small vessels were contacted by radar. During the approach *Tang* was detected by an escort at a range of 7,000 yards and forced to deep submergence. Five depth charges were dropped in a half hearted attack and the escort continued on. Fifteen minutes later *Tang* resumed the approach at radar depth in spite of additional depth charges in the vicinity, dropped at random by escorts. The range was closed to 1,000 yards and three hits of four torpedoes fired sank a freighter. *Tang* cleared the area at deep submergence undetected. An attempt was made to again get ahead of the convoy for a dawn attack, but the remaining freighter passed out of range under cover of air escort.

(B) During the night of 22 February two night surface attacks were made on a convoy of three freighters with a destroyer and three smaller escorts. In each attack four torpedoes were fired at close range, one resulting in four hits and the other in three. Both targets quickly sank. Tang evaded on the surface. During the following day the remnants of this convoy could not be found.

(C) About 1100, 24 February a tanker, a freighter, and a destroyer were sighted at about 12 miles. Effort to gain satisfactory position for day periscope attack was unsuccessful, because of rain squalls and the wide zig zags of the targets. Contact was maintained and a night surface attack with four torpedoes resulted in three good hits which destroyed the freighter. *Tang* retired on the surface amid enemy shell fire and random depth charges. Contact with the tanker and destroyer was maintained and position gained for dawn attack submerged. Decks of the tanker were covered with lookouts as three of the four torpedoes fired hit and sank this ship in four minutes. A counter-attack followed without damage to the *Tang* although the evasion tactics were hampered by the necessity of pumping bilges and blowing safety tank, because a torpedo tube outer door gasket had been blown out and the inner door gasket rolled out of its groove under pressure.

(D) The final attack was made after moonset on 26 February after a late afternoon contact had been made and the enemy tracked. A transport, a freighter and four escorts made up the convoy. *Tang* maneuvered into position on the wildly zig zagging transport and fired four torpedoes at a range of 1,600 yards. All missed astern apparently due to an increase of enemy speed. The approach and retirement were made on the surface.

4.   The material condition of the *Tang* is excellent. It is expected that the refit will be completed in ten days. Consideration should be given to the replacement of torpedo tube door gaskets with T-shaped gaskets in the future.

5.   The Commanding Officer, officers and crew of the *Tang* are heartily congratulated on this very aggressive and successful first patrol and the excellent start they have given this new ship. It is recommended that the following damage inflicted on the enemy be credited to the *Tang*:

SUNK

1 – Freighter (*Hansei Maru* class)	7,700 tons
1 – Freighter (*Kenyo Maru* class)	6,486 tons
1 – Naval Auxiliary (*Arimason Maru* class)	8,696 tons
1 – Freighter (*Tatutake Maru* class)	7,068 tons
1 – Tanker	18,276 tons

C.C. Smith

A16-3/   Commander Submarine Force, Pacific Fleet   (Nc)
                    Subordinate Command, Navy No. 1504.
Serial No. 050
                              Care of Fleet Post Office,
C-O-N-F-I-D-E-N-T-I-A-L   San Francisco, California,
                                    5 March 1944.
Second Endorsement to
U.S.S. *Tang* Report of
First War Patrol.

From: Commander Submarine Force, Pacific Fleet,
                    Subordinate Command, Navy No. 1504
To: The Commander-in-Chief, United States Fleet
Via: (1) The Commander Submarine Force, Pacific Fleet
               (2) The Commander-in-Chief, United States Pacific Fleet

Subject: U.S.S. *Tang* – Report of First War Patrol.

1.   Forwarded.
2.   The first war patrol of the *Tang* can only be classified as outstanding. Of the six attacks made, five were made on consecutive days. Five of the attacks resulted in destruction of the target and tremendous damage was inflicted on the enemy.
3.   The Commander Submarine Force, Pacific Fleet, Subordinate Command adds his congratulations to the Commanding Officer, officers and crew on this outstanding first patrol and concurs in the summation of damage dealt to the enemy, as contained in the first endorsement.

C.D. Edmunds.

FF12-10/A16-3(15)/(12)   Submarine Force, Pacific Fleet   nr

Serial 0473   Care of Fleet Post Office,
                                                   San Francisco, California,
<u>CONFIDENTIAL</u>   11 March 1944.

<u>Third Endorsement</u> to   Note: This report will be
Tang Report of   destroyed prior to
First War Patrol   entering patrol area.

ComSubPac Patrol Report No. 380
U.S.S. *Tang* – First War Patrol

From: The Commander Submarine Force, Pacific Fleet.
To: The Commander-in-Chief, United States Fleet.
Via: The Commander-in-Chief, U.S. Pacific Fleet.

Subject: U.S.S. *Tang* (SS306) – Report of First War Patrol.
            (22 January to 3 March 1944).

    1.   The first war patrol of the *Tang* was also the first for the Commanding Officer, as such. The patrol was conducted in the Caroline and Marianas Islands area.

    2.   Six outstanding attacks were made during this patrol, all of which were extremely well planned, determined and aggressive, resulting in severe damage to the enemy.

    3.   Sixteen hits out of 24 torpedoes fired is most commendable, and adequately shows the excellence of the *Tang*'s fire control party.

    4.   This patrol is designated as successful for Combat Insignia Award.

    5.   The Commander Submarine Force, Pacific Fleet, congratulates the Commanding Officer, officers, and crew for this well planned, aggressive, and very successful war patrol. The *Tang* is credited with inflicting the following damage upon the enemy:

SUNK

1 – Freighter (*Hansei Maru* class)	–	7,770 tons (Attack No. 1)
1 – Freighter (*Kenyo Maru* class)	–	6,468 tons (Attack No. 2)
1 – Submarine Tender	–	8,663 tons (Attack No. 3)
1 – Freighter (*Tatutaki Maru* class)	–	7,068 tons (Attack No. 4)
1 – Naval Tanker	–	<u>12,000</u> tons (Attack No. 5)
	Total	41,969 tons

J.H. Brown, Jr.

Distribution:
(Complete Reports)

Cominch	(5)
CNO	(5)
Cincpac	(6)
Intel.Cen.Pac.Ocean Areas	(1)
Comservpac	
(Adv. Base Plan. Unit)	(1)
Cinclant	(2)
Comsublant	(8)
S/M School, NL	(2)
Comsopac	(1)
Comsowepac	(1)
CTF 72	(2)
Comnorpac	(1)
Comsubpac	(40)
SUBAD, MI	(2)
ComsubpacSubordcom	(3)
All Squadron and Div.	
Commanders, Subspac	(2)
Comsubstrainpac	(2)
All Submarines, Subspac	(1)

E.L. Hymes, II.
Flag Secretary.

Patrol Two, 16 March 1944 – 15 May 1944

U.S.S. *Tang* (SS306)
c/o Fleet Post Office
San Francisco, California

SS306/A16-3
Serial 09   May 15, 1944.
CONFIDENTIAL

From: The Commanding Officer
To: The Commander in Chief, United States Fleet
Via: The Commander Submarine Division 141
               The Commander Submarine Squadron 14
               The Commander Submarine Force Pacific Fleet
               The Commander in Chief, U.S. Pacific Fleet

Subject: U.S.S. *Tang* (SS306), Report of War Patrol #2

Enclosure: (A) Subject Report.
               (B) Track Charts. (ComSubPac only).

1.   Enclosure (A), covering the second war patrol of this vessel conducted in areas northeast of Palau, east of Davao, and at Truk, during the period 16 March 1944 to 15 May 1944, is forwarded herewith.

R.H. O'Kane

(A) PROLOGUE

Returned from first patrol March third and complete refit on the eleventh. As no difficulties were expected or experienced, post repair was combined with two day and one night training period. Finished loading on the fifteenth, and departed on second patrol at dawn March sixteenth.

(B) NARRATIVE

March 16 (-12)
0655 Left Midway for Palau, proceeding at two engine speed.

March 17 (-11)
Enroute area conducting routine drills and dives.

March 23 (-11)
0512 Sighted trawler on patrol and avoided on the surface. Our position, 150 miles west of Pagan Island, indicates that this vessel probably was a spotter, and not fishing.
1235 Dived for half an hour on sighting an unidentified plane.
1712 Dived until dusk to avoid being sighted while passing between Pagan and Alamagan Islands. Delayed an hour to insure peak radar operation while we had land contacts available. In spite of the excellent wave meters and other apparatus now provided for tuning this equipment, there is nothing like a good land contact to demonstrate its proper operation. Even the experts concede this.

March 24 (-10)
0907 Changed course to north to intercept U.S.S. *Barb*'s convoy.
1406 Dived for thirty minutes to avoid a patrol type aircraft.
1608 Dived for two SD contacts at ten miles.
1632 Surfaced and proceeded along reverse of expected convoy track until dark, and then proceeded toward assigned area west of Palau, as our orders will not permit further delay.

March 25-26 (-9)
Enroute area.

March 27 (-9)
1651 Dived and avoided an unidentified aircraft.

2000 Entered area 10W, then proceeded to position sixty miles bearing 255° from Toagel Mlungui pass, as assigned for strike on Palau.

March 28 (-9)

On assigned station. Conducted submerged patrol as ordered, but searching continuously with 17 feet of both periscopes, sound, and guarding 450 KC on the SD mast.

March 29 (-9)

Patrolling submerged as on previous day.

1210 Sighted patrol type plane.

1823 Just prior to surfacing, sighted thin round mast of a ship. Conducted submerged approach at six knots until dark but could not close it sufficiently to determine its identity.

1857 Surfaced, continued tracking, and took position ahead for moonlight submerged observation and possible firing, although the "blurb" of the target at 7,000 yards seemed very small.

1950 Almost simultaneously with lightning flashes which revealed the target to be a PC type patrol, six large planes in groups of two arrived on the scene. They had on both running lights and landing lights and proceeded with what appeared to be a routine submarine search. As we were in an unfortunate position ahead of the first PC, which was later joined by a second, it required two hours at periscope depth and finally deep submergence to get clear.

March 30 (-9)

Conducted submerged patrol, searching with seven feet of periscope.

1217 Heard a good explosion, followed by a second fifteen seconds later. As the horizon was absolutely clear,

1227 surfaced for a better look.

1258 Sighted three planes, believed friendly, simultaneous with radar contact at seven miles. Dived and continued submerged patrol.

March 31 (-9)

Patrolled submerged on assigned station.

0721 Sighted bomber, fairly close.

1700 Sighted medium bomber on easterly course.

2232 Sighted two planes on the SD at about 16 miles which bothered us for half an hour as they conducted a search under the half moon. As they did not close inside eight miles, remained on the surface.

April 1 (-9)

0553 Sighted a large plane on the horizon, dived and commenced usual high periscope submerged patrol for the day.

April 2 (-9)

0104 Sighted flash over horizon on bearing of Palau, followed by apparent loom of searchlights.

0553 Commenced submerged high periscope patrol.

2000 Departed at one engine speed for newly assigned station 120-150 miles east of Davao City, Mindanao.

April 3 (-9)

0100 Passed to operational command of ComTaskFor Seventy-One.

0808 Dived for one half hour and apparently avoided detection by a patrol plane.

2400 Entered new area east of Davao Gulf.

April 4 (-9)

Patrolled on surface in center of assigned area, searching with both periscopes, sound to detect echo ranging and SJ during reduced visibility.

0847 Dived for three-quarters of an hour and apparently avoided detection by a plane sighted on SD at twelve miles.

April 5 (-9)

Searched on surface as on previous day.

1042 Dived for forty minutes and apparently avoided detection by a plane sighted on the horizon.

April 6 (-9)

Patrolling on surface.

2100 Departed area, proceeding east at five knots on the auxiliary engine to conserve fuel. Our number 4 MBT could not be converted by Submarine Base, Midway, during the last refit.

April 7 (-9)

0752 Dived for twenty minutes and avoided plane sighted on horizon, then proceeded toward former area at five knots, searching as usual with everything we've got.

0900 Passed to operational command of ComTaskFor Seventeen.

April 8 (-9)

Patrolling on the surface enroute newest area northwest of Palau.

0900 Commenced passing through a field of oil drums which continued throughout the day.

1500 SJ radar out of commission on afternoon test. The radar officer, radio technician, and leading radioman were relieved of all other duties and commenced "round the clock" repairs.

April 9 (-9)

0330 Sighted an unidentified plane which did not close, so continued on the surface. Numerous oil drums were again in sight all day.

April 10 (-9)

0058 Sighted plane on SD radar which closed to five miles before opening.

0813 Dived for forty minutes for a plane on SD at 8 miles. Apparently avoided detection due to overcast skys.

1017 Sighted single mast and deck house of an apparent PC type patrol boat. Dived and attempted to close to investigate, but height of eye range and change of bearing, when next observed from forty feet, showed him on a northeasterly course, at better than fifteen knots, and out of reach. As we were then about fifty miles from Toagel Mlungui pass, and expecting shipping within a day, continued on submerged to close the island undetected, but searching with 17 feet of periscope. It was a long haul from Mindanao on the auxiliary engine, but otherwise we would not have had sufficient fuel to complete the patrol.

April 11 (-9)

Conducted submerged patrol ten miles west of Ngaruangl passage, with periodic high periscope searches. From this position we would have been able to intercept shipping through this passage or around Velasco reef, headed for Toagel Mlungui, and at the same time, been able to spot and trail for night attack any traffic from this latter pass. We considered this our first "likely spot" in nearly four weeks of patrol.

April 12 (-9)

As the *Trigger* was delayed in entering her lower half of area 10 NW, patrolled submerged five miles off Toagel Mlungui passage, covering her area as well as our own.

April 13 (-9)

Conducted submerged patrol between three and four miles off Toagel Mlungui.

1220 Sighted four motored flying boat which apparently landed in the lagoon. Repairs were completed to the SJ today, and it worked with peak performance on surfacing. As we have patrolled close in and enjoyed bright nights, it is doubtful that any shipping slipped by us, especially as Toagel Mlungui pass would hardly be used at night, unlighted.

April 14 (-9)
0154 Sighted U.S.S. *Trigger* on the SJ radar, as she crossed our area. Closed her and made preliminary arrangements for mutual assistance in covering this area, and established sound communications for later use.

Patrolled two miles off Toagel Mlungui during forenoon.

1400 As passing squalls developed into steady rain, surfaced, moved out to five miles from the pass, and conducted radar search. After dark, moved out to contact *Trigger*, but SJ failure prevented early rendezvous.

April 15 (-9)
0011 Sighted U.S.S. *Trigger*, and sent over the following by the tin can-line throwing gun method: (1) All new information we have concerning this area. (2) Our ideas for its most effective coverage by two submarines. (3) A duplicate copy of coordinated attack doctrine and signals for possible use. Received compatable ideas for coordinated patrol, and a report of *Trigger*'s super convoy and her damage, for delivery to ComSubPac. Returned to Toagel Mlungui before dawn and conducted submerged patrol three to four miles off pass during the day.

1056 Sighted four engine flying boat.

1638 Sighted four engine bomber.

2152 Made rendezvous with *Trigger* who sent a rubber boat to *Tang*. Supplied her with compressor valves and cages, radar tubes, and our spare battery blower motor to use as a sound training motor.

April 16 (-9)
Patrolled submerged two to three miles off Toagel Mlungui.

0740 Sighted bomber.

1400 As *Trigger* was patrolling out today, proceeded southwest about three miles off the reef to investigate lower lagoon and western entrance to Malakal Harbor. No evidence of any shipping could be detected.

1552 Sighted bomber over lagoon.

April 17 (-9)
Patrolled submerged three miles of Toagel Mlungui.

1215 Sighted large flying boat which apparently landed in lagoon.

April 18 (-9)

Patrolled submerged of Toagel Mlungui.

1013 Sighted flying boat over lagoon.

2130 Made rendezvous with *Trigger*. Sent over compressor valves to her and exchanged spare SJ modulator units in hopes of fixing our ailing SJ radar.

Completed repairs during the night.

April 19 (-9)

Patrolled in same vicinity as on previous day, withdrawing as usual to the northwest during the night to insure a night radar run on any inbound convoy.

April 20 (-9)

Patrolled as on previous day.

0750 Sighted flying boat.

April 21 (-9)

Patrolled three miles off Toagel Mlungui pass.

0619 Sighted bomber on westerly course.

April 22 (-9)

0439 Sighted searchlight over the horizon in vicinity of harbor.

0504 Commenced submerged patrol closing to former position off Toagel Mlungui.

1143 Sighted five bombers flying south over the island.

1305 Sighted another bomber over lagoon headed west.

1440 Sighted flight of six bombers over the island.

2040 Departed for area fifteen to perform lifeguard services, proceeding at one engine speed. Though we regretted leaving this area without making our presence felt, our observations lead us to believe that it will remain stagnant for some time and that our route to Truk will offer better chance of contact.

April 23 (-9)

Enroute Truk at one engine speed, searching with both periscopes, sound to detect echo ranging, and SJ radar during passing squalls.

1840 In anticipation of bombarding the phosphorite refinery on Fais Island the following evening, commenced firing seven rounds to determine the limiting point of twilight for accurate pointing and training, and to establish the ballistic[s] to make the sight bar range equal radar range to the splashes.

April 24 (-9)

0600 As we were sufficiently ahead of schedule, changed course to close Fais Island, forty miles north of our track.

1000 Dived fifteen miles from the island and closed at four knots. As we were aware of the reported gun emplacements, established the bearing line between lookout tower and refinery as 128° T, then proceeded around the island for bombardment by indirect fire. Surfaced in evening twilight with lookout tower, our point of aim,

1828 bearing 308° T, range 7,300 yards, and commenced firing 33 rounds of four inch. To insure crossing the refinery, employed a rocking leader of 200 and then 100 yard steps, and applied deflection spots as previously computed to include other structures in the installation. Though the results were not discernable, the shell detonations were nicely visible at the bottom of the ladders and the target area was crossed several times. As expected, their guns, placed to protect the installation on the west side of the island, were unable to return any fire.

1845 Set course for new lifeguard station off Truk at one engine speed.

April 25-26 (-10)

Enroute Truk.

April 27 (-10)

0859 Dived for a six mile SD contact simultaneous with high periscope sighting of smoke to the southwest near Hitchfield Bank. On return to periscope depth eight minutes later, sighted the plane going away, and then the smoke from fifty feet. There were two patches tracked on a westerly course at about ten knots. Our attempts to "end around" before the enemy might reach Grey Feather Bank were frustrated by the air coverage which drove us down five times before noon, the last with a "swish," perhaps of a dub bomb, and a rattle of machine gun bullets. Continued trailing for three more hours, but sighted no more smoke. The enemy was now an hour on the bank, and a hundred mile chase faced us with no assurance that we could guess where he would again strike deep water. Faced with this and the problem of reaching our lifeguard station by the following day, regretfully set course for Truk.

April 28 (-10)

0714 Dived on border of assigned area northwest of Truk, and apparently avoided detection by a distant twin engine bomber. Continued high periscope submerged patrol throughout the day.

1522 Sighted distant plane on easterly course in direction of island.

1718 Sighted two float planes.

1859 Shortly after surfacing dived for a six mile SD contact which closed slowly to two miles. Remained submerged for an hour.

April 29 (-10)

Conducted submerged high periscope patrol, working around to lifeguard position east of Truk for strike from Marshalls.

0550 Sighted float plane fairly close.

1928 About a half hour after surfacing commenced tracking attacking Liberators which passed seven miles north of us enroute Truk, which was thirty miles distant.

1950 Observed several explosions in direction of island.

2000 Commenced diving at approximately one hour intervals to avoid a determined search of the area along our bearing from Truk. As our bearing was 110° T from Dublon, quite to the south of the track of Liberators returning to Eniwetok or other Marshalls base, it was at once considered that this search was for us. Their search consisted of dropping increasing numbers of flares as they approached us from the island, employing three to four planes. The closest flares were about five miles distant. The plane contacts would continue to close to from three to four miles where they would fade out, most probably as the searchers came low to locate us by silhouette, for dead in the water we were probably invisible from overhead. Naturally we dived at this point of their search. After three such dives we had moved out to forty miles from the island and were no longer troubled, although moonset may have caused them to give up. It certainly appeared that the planes were vectored out along our bearing and that they did not know our distance from the island. Further, our distances check with data concerning the DF'ing of the SD radar received subsequently.

April 30 (-10)

On surface in assigned position for carrier strikes on Truk, 40 miles bearing 180° T from Moen Island.

0400 Sighted strong radar interference on the SJ on beam bearing 240° T, obviously from our approaching task force.

0436 Sighted low flying plane or planes on SJ radar, which passed 4,600 yards from us headed toward our task force.

0530 Sighted first planes on SD.

0610 Watched plane go down in flames over Dublon Island.

0630 Dived for thirteen minutes and avoided a group of possibly unfriendly planes which closed rapidly to two miles.

0643 On surfacing, flights of up to fifty planes were continuously shuttling between Truk and the southwest. With the possible exception of a sinking *Maru*, this was the most encouraging sight we've witnessed in this war to date.

0815 Sighted tops, then superstructure of our task force.

1025 Received first report of downed plane and headed for reported position two miles of Fourup Island at emergency speed. Bombers working over Fourup and Ollan Islands were most reassuring, and with numerous fighters to guide us, located the life raft promptly about four miles west of its reported position.

1156 With Lieutenant (junior grade) S. Scammell, USN, J. D. Gendron, AMM2c, and H.B. Gemmell, ARM2c on board, withdrew six miles to the south.

1559 Proceeded at emergency speed on a course to round Kuop Islands to reach life raft outside the reef on the east side of Truk. Fifteen minutes later however a second raft was reported to the north of us in the approximate position of our first recovery. As the latter could be reached during daylight, returned at emergency speed to this position two miles east of Ollan and one mile off the reef. The hovering bomber and two fighters seemed perturbed that we wouldn't follow them over to the actual position, some five miles inside the reef. As a twenty minute search with periscopes and from atop the shears did not locate the raft, headed south again to carry out the original plan. All planes had now been recalled, leaving us a bit naked, so to avoid a prolonged submerged retirement, opened fire with 4" H.E. on the gun emplacements on the southwest end of Ollan Island. Our ballistic of the previous week again proved correct, for with sight bar range 300 yards less than radar range, the first shell burst nicely low in the trees intended to conceal the emplacements. Fired twenty round of H.E. and common while retiring, quite agreeably amazed at the ability of the 4" to stay on the target. Corrected radar range fed continuously to the gun, with occasional salvos spotted short, appears a simple and adequate means of fire control. At 3,500 yards trained in and turned tail, a bit prematurely, however, for the nips crawled out of their holes and let fly at us. Their first splash was about 1,000 yards short,

1850 the second we didn't spot. Remained submerged for forty minutes, then surfaced and proceeded toward east side of Truk at emergency speed.

2143 From position six miles east of Feinif Island on the eastern reef, commenced zigzag search to the southwest at ten knots. Fired green Very stars every fifteen minutes at the turns and midway of each leg, hoping for any sort of answer from one of the rafts. The only reply, sighted on some occasions, was a series of red or white lights in the neighborhood of Uman Island, which changed bearing rapidly as if flashed along a runway. One of the pilots we recovered the following day had sighted our stars, but was afraid to answer them

May 1 (-10)

0330 Proceeded east to a position for second day's strike, ten miles closer to the Island than on the previous day.

0340 Sighted radar interference of our task force.

0600 Sighted conning tower of jap submarine proceeding south around Kuop from Otta pass. Submerged and commenced approach. Tracked him on straight course 180° at 12 knots. When the generated range was 3,000 yards and angle on the bow 30 starboard, suddenly lost sound contact. Took a quick look to observe our bombers and fighters overhead and to confirm our fears that the enemy had dived. Dropped to 150 feet and rigged for silent running, but was unable to regain contact. Headed southwest for an hour at standard speed, then surfaced and proceeded to the northwest toward the reported raft of the evening before. Spread large colors on deck to help identify us, then reported enemy sub to the task force commander for possible attack.

0828 Headed at emergency speed for life raft reported two and a half miles southwest of our favorite Ollan Island. Before we reached the scene, a float plane from the U.S.S. *North Carolina* capsized in the cross chop in the attempt to rescue. The other *North Carolina* plane made a precarious landing and on our arrival was towing both raft and fellow pilot clear of the island. This action was most helpful, for we expected competition from Ollan, and nearby fighters were already strafing her gun emplacements for us.

0917 After Lieutenant J.J. Dowdle, USNR, Lieutenant (junior grade) P. Kanze, for whom we had searched the night before, and R.E. Hill, ARM2c, were on board, and the second plane from the *North Carolina* had somehow gotten into the air again, we proceeded to sink the capsized plane from the *North Carolina* had somehow gotten into the air again, we proceeded to sink the capsized plane with 20 MM fire. At this time a smoking torpedo bomber was spotted hitting the water about seven miles to the east. Proceeded down the bearing at emergency speed, and opened fire on nearby Ollan as we passed. They had removed the trees intended to camouflage their position, evidently feeling it was no longer a secret. It gave us an unobstructed point of aim, however, and our hitting 4" H.E. with a few common sandwiched in, supported by strafing fighters and topped off with two bombers, must have discouraged them for they did not return any fire.

1004 Sighted life raft and survivors ahead under circling fighters.

1020 With Commander A.R. Matter, USN, J.J. Lenahan, ARM2c, and H.A. Thompson, ACM2c, on board, proceeded at emergency speed to round Kuop to reach three life rafts reported off the eastern reef. As our track took us close by our submarine contact of the morning, requested and promptly got good air coverage. Blown high, with safety, negative and the fuel group dry, and even our Fairbanks-Morse smoking a bit, rolled through this spot at 21 knots fairly confident that the jap would get no more than a fleeting glimpse. As Lieut(jg) Burns had landed his *North Carolina* float plane off the eastern reef, requested that he attempt to tow the rafts clear. He was a big jump ahead of us however, having taken all seven men from three rafts

1328 on board and taxied with them to seaward. They were now in no immediate danger, so followed our escorting planes to a raft just off Mesegon Island in the bight between Kuop and Truk. As we thoroughly expected to be driven down, rigged a free running line and life ring to the SD mast for towing the raft clear while submerged, but our strafing escorts evidently discouraged any opposition.

1325 Recovered Lieutenant H.E. Hill, USNR, then headed for a fighter pilot reported in the water just off the

1352 eastern reef of Kuop. By the time of our arrival planes had dropped a rubber boat to him, but he was too weak to do more than climb aboard one.

1410 After pulling perhaps our most grateful passenger aboard, Lieutenant (junior grade) J.G. Cole, USNR, backed up wind clear of the reef and headed for the waiting float plane at emergency speed. She was well clear, about three miles east of Salat Island, and no difficulty was experienced in bringing the following on board: Lieutenant R.S. Nelson, USNR; Lieutenant (junior grade) R. Barbor, USNR; Lieutenant (junior grade) J.A. Burns, USNR; Ensign C.L. Farrell, USNR; J. Livingston, ARM1c; R.W. Gruebel, AMM2c; J. Hranek, ARM2c; O.F. Tabrun, AMM2c; and R. Hill, ARM2c. The action of Lieut(jg) Burns, in making the rescue possible by deliberately placing himself in as precarious a position as any of the downed personnel, will be made the subject of a special report.

1515 Sank the float plane, which had a flooded battered tail, with 20 MM fire, and proceeded at emergency speed to round Kuop to the last reported raft south of Ollan Island. As all planes were recalled as of 1630, and we could not reach the raft until sunset, requested two night fighters to assist in locating it. Our passage through the area of our morning contact was not quite as comfortable without air coverage, but again twenty-one knots took us through in a hurry. The night fighters joined us at sunset as we were approaching the last reported position three and a half mile south of Ollan, and immediately commenced their search. Fifteen minutes later one of the fighters circled then fired several red Very stars four miles northwest of us. Closed at emergency speed, spotting the raft from atop the shears, as it was now too dark for periscopes.

1830 With Lieutenant D. Kirkpatrick, USNR, and R.L. Bently, AOM2c, on board, dismissed the planes and commenced slow speed search west of the atoll.

May 2 (-10)

Conducted submerged high periscope search off the western reef.

0955 Sighted flying boat over the lagoon.

1135 Sighted land plane near Tol Island.

1211 Sighted patrol plane in the west on a northerly course.

1220 Sighted probably same patrol on easterly course.

1605 Sighted unidentified aircraft in the northwest, headed for Truk.

2005 Sighted A/A fire and explosions on Truk from Liberator raid.

May 3 (-10)

Searched as on previous day.

1725 Sighted float plane headed west.

May 4 (-10)

Conducted submerged high periscope patrol in most likely spot to intercept traffic for Otta pass. Conducted search after dark, retiring to vicinity of Otta pass for submerged patrol.

May 5 (-10)

Conducted submerged patrol off Otaa pass.

0615 Sighted float plane to the south.

After dark proceeded outside forty mile circle to position east of Dublon for Liberator strike on Truk.

May 6 (-10)

0056 Several planes passed seven to twelve miles from us, tracked by SD radar.

0110 Sighted radar interference of U.S.S. *Permit* entering area.

0116 Observed explosions on bearing of Dublon.

0200 Though all large plane contacts had disappeared, we were again bothered by searchers which maintained contact with us for another hour. We stopped and headed up the moon streak when they came within five miles, and avoided the closest one at three miles in a rain squall. The three pips then moved out to seven and finally twelve miles, and then disappeared.

0300 With all planes departed and our relief in the area, set course for Pearl at two engine speed on prescribed routing.

0557 Three quarters of an hour after our trim dive, submerged for twenty minutes and avoided a float plane, probably searching from the Hall Islands, fifty miles distant. Had two plane contacts outside thirty miles during remainder of day. After dark, sent message concerning airmen aboard.

May 7 (-10)
Enroute Pearl.

0701 Tracked plane at forty miles on SD for some minutes.

0825 Dived for twenty minutes to avoid a large low flying plane.

1202 Tracked plane in from 14 miles.

1204 Target sighted and identified as a PBM at eight miles, dived as his approach was menacing.

1500 SJ radar out of commission on afternoon test. The last modulator unit, obtained from *Trigger*, has also leaked its oil. Commenced round the clock repairs.

1800 Held demonstration of all identification flares and stars (ex-smoke bombs) for the benefit of the aviators on board, none of whom had seen them before.

May 8 (-11)
Enroute Pearl.

May 9 (-11)

0513 In position 120 miles from Wake, dived for plane sighted on the SD which closed rapidly from 10 to 7 miles. Though our position is nearly on a line between Eniewetok and Wake, it is doubtful that a friendly plane would be here at dawn.

1137 Sighted plane on SD which closed from 17 to 12 miles before opening.

1300 Slowed to one engine to conserve fuel.

(C) WEATHER

The weather was normal for the areas and periods covered.

(D) TIDAL INFORMATION

The tidal conditions were normal.

(E) NAVIGATIONAL AIDS

None sighted.

(F) SHIP CONTACTS

See page 16. [p. 40]

(G) AIRCRAFT CONTACTS

See page 17-19 [41-42]

(H) ATTACK DATA

No attacks.

(I) MINES

None observed.

(J) ANTI-SUBMARINE AND EVASION TACTICS

Extensive use of aircraft was bothersome day and night. It is not believed that any were radar equipped, but some were obviously searching along our bearing from Truk as noted in the narrative, most probably as a result of DF'ing our SD. Off Palau a combined aircraft and surface search was encountered which was avoided at deep submergence below a 26° gradient.

(K) MAJOR DEFECTS AND DAMAGE

None.

Ship Contacts

No.	Date	Time	Lat	Long	Type	Initial Range	Est. Course	Est. Speed	How Cont.	Remarks
1.	3-23-44	0512	18-40 N	148-30 E	Fishing Patrol	5,000	Various	Unknown	Sight	Evaded on surface
2.	3-29-44	1823	7-10 N	133-25 E	Patrols 2	14,000	090	8	Periscope	Tracked then evaded.
3.	4-10-44	1030	8-25 N	134-05 E	Patrol	20,000		13	Periscope Surface	Disappeared over horizon
4.	4-24-44	0900	6-50 N	148-50 E	Smoke (2)	30,000	270	10	Periscope Surface	Sub forced down 5 times by air contact.
5.	5-1-44	0800	7-10 N	151-45 E	Submarine RO class	14,000	180	12	Surface Periscope	Sub dived for our planes.

Aircraft Contacts

No	Date	Time	Latitude	Longitude	Type	Initial Range	Est. Course	Est. Alt.	How Cont.	Remarks
1.	3-23-44	1235	18-15 N	147-00 E	Unknown	10 mi.		1,000	Sight	
2.	3-24-44	1406	17-37 N	143-45 E	Patrol	10 mi.	140 T	1,000	Sight	
3.	3-24-44	1608	18-03 N	143-41 E	Not Sighted	10 mi			Radar	Two cont. close together
4.	3-27-44	1651	09-30 N	133-05 E	Unknown	5 mi.	045 T		Sight	
5.	3-29-44	1210	07-21 N	133-24 E	Patrol	8 mi.	050 T	1,000	Periscope	
6.	3-29-44	1950	07-10 N	133-60 E	Unknown (6)	Various			Running lights	Large
7.	3-30-44	1258	07-18 N	133-31 E	Unknown (3)	7 mi.	135 T		Radar & sight	Probably friendly
8.	3-31-44	0721	07-13 N	133-08 E	Twin tail twin eng.	2 mi.	070 T	200	Periscope	Light underneath
9.	3-31-44	1700	07-13 N	133-08 E	Medium bomber 2 eng.	6 mi.	090 T	500	Periscope	Low wing monoplane
10.	3-31-44	2230	07-16 N	133-31 E		17 mi.			SD	2 contacts
11.	4-1-44	0553	07-20 N	133-42 E	2 eng. medium bomber	7 mi.	095 T	1,000	Bridge Lookout	Dark paint
12.	4-3-44	0308	07-17 N	131-28 E	Float type	8 mi	121 T	900	Bridge lookout	Small
13.	4-4-44	0847	07-41 N	127-41 E	Radar cont.	12 mi.			SD	Dove to 150'
14.	4-4-44	0847	07-41 N	127-41 E	Flying boat	4 mi.		200	Sight	
15.	4-5-44	1042	06-42 N	172-41 E	Unident.	9 mi.			Sight	Dove to 150'
16.	4-10-44	0058	08-40 N	133-35 E	Unident.	6 mi.			Radar	
17.	4-10-44	0813	03-35 N	134-00 E	Unident.	8 mi.			Radar	
18.	4-10-44	1220	07-39 N	134-24 E	Flying boat	14 mi.	130 T	500	Periscope	Landed Rose-ball Lagoon
19.	4-15-44	1056	07-38 N	134-25 E	Flying boat	3 mi.	160 T		Periscope	Dove to 150'
20.	4-15-44	1638	07-38 N	134-25 E	Bomber	3 mi.	150 T	1,000	Periscope	Plane headed for [illegible]
21.	4-16-44	0640	07-36 N	134-23 E	Bomber	3 mi.	270 T	1,000	Periscope	Outbound
22.	4-16-44	1652	07-28 N	134-19 E	Bomber	5 mi.	040	1,000	Periscope	Outbound
23.	4-17-44	1215	07-34 N	134-23 E	Flying Boat	6 mi.	Circ. for landing	500	Periscope	Inbound

#	Date	Time	Lat	Lon	Type	Distance	Bearing	Altitude	Method	Notes
24.	4-18-44	1015	07-39 N	134-25 E	2 motor flying boat	7 mi.		1,000 down	Periscope	Inbound
25.	4-22-44	0620	07-43 N	134-20 E	2 eng. Bomber	8 mi.	070 T	800	Lookout	Twin tail
26.	4-22-44	1145	07-37 N	134-24 E	"	7 mi.	190 T	800	Periscope	5 in formation
27.	4-22-44	1305	07-36 N	134-24 E	Land bomber	4 mi.	230 T	900	Periscope	
28.	4-22-44	1340	07-36 N	134-25 E	(6) Bombers	20 mi.	100 T	1,050	Periscope	6 in formation
29.	4-23-44	1643	09-05 N	137-12 E	Bomber	15 mi.	257 T			
30.	4-25-44	1445	09-02 N	143-45 E	2 bomber	10 mi.	220		Sight	Doubtful
31.	4-27-44	0900	06-50 N	146-50 E	Fighter	6 mi.	220	SD 1,000	Periscope	
32.	4-28-44	0705	06-55 N	151-05 E	Bomber	15 mi.	North	1,000	Lookout	
33.	4-28-44	0705	06-55 N	151-05 E	Flying boat	20 mi.			Periscope	
34.	4-28-44	1537	"	"	"	"			"	Possibly same as 34 [*sic*]
35.	4-28-44	1718	06-55 N	151-05 E	Sea plane	1 mi.	South	800	Periscope	
36.	4-29-44	0550	06-50 N	156-00 E	"	½ mi.	[south]	500	Periscope	
37.	4-29-44	1900 2400	06-50 N	152-52 E	Many unident.	2-14 mi			Radar Sight	Many planes
38.	4-30-44	All Day	06-50 N	151-52 E	Many					Many planes
39.	5-1-44	All Day	06-50 N	151-52 E	Many	0-14 mi			" "	" "
40.	5-2-44	1000	07-15 N	152-35 E	Flying boat	6 mi.	120 T		Periscope	
41.	5-2-44		07-15 N	152-35 E	Zeke	3 mi.	090 T		Periscope	
42.	5-2-44	1605	07-10 N	152-35 E	SB	12 mi.	090 T	1,000	Periscope	Entering Truk
43.	5-3-44	1725	07-20 N	151-20 E	Recc	10 mi.	270 T	1,000	Periscope	Similar to (SOC3)
44.	5-4-44	1030	07-05 N	150-28 E	Unident	7 mi.	090 T	500	Sight	
45.	5-5-44	0615	07-08 N	151-45 E	Recc	10 mi.	225 T	1,500	Periscope	SOC3 type
46.	5-6-44	0100	07-45 N	151-35 E		15 mi.			Radar	Many
47.	5-6-44	0355	08-40 N	153-00 E	Dave	12 mi.	090	2,000	Sight	
48.	5-7-44	0000	12-50 N	156-10 E		15 mi.	200	1,000	Sight	
49.	5-7-44	0820	12-55 N	156-30 E		8 mi.		Low	Sight	Dove to 150'
50.	5-7-44	1205	13-35 N	156-45 E	PBM	11 mi.		High	SD Sight	Avoided
51	5-9-44	0512	17-47 N	166-30 E		7 mi.			SD	Dove to 150'

(L) RADIO

Radio reception was good and no difficulty was experienced in any transmissions. Of special note was the very satisfactory two way voice communication during the strike on Truk in part due to the wardroom Hallicrafter receiver. The frequency of 4475 could be answered by all planes and had the advantage of being clear of their VHF tactical frequency. It was therefore possible for planes to direct us quickly, and for us to get their support when needed. Voice on the RL receiver was quite often unintelligible.

(M) RADAR

The performance of the SJ radar was very satisfactory when it was in operation. Fortunately its off periods in general coincided with bright nights when shipping could be sighted and to the return trip. The trouble was generally in the new type transmitter and among other things entailed the failure of the original modulator unit, the spare, and finally a third obtained from the U.S.S. *Trigger.* Around the clock repairs by our "long course" radar officer, a first class radio technician, and a first class radioman could only temporarily overcome the rate of breakdown. A thousand man hours were devoted exclusively to its overhaul with only temporary results and the knowledge that "they hadn't said uncle" as a reward. The details of the failure are listed below:

Item Number	Description	Number of Failures	Reason for Failure
135	VR-150/30 Tube	2	Lost Gas
120	6L6 (metal) Tube	4	Shorted and weak
121	6L6 (glass) Tube	1	Poor emission
134	VS-105/30 Tube	1	Lost Gas
140	919 LP Lamps	4	Poor regulation
117	6AC7 Tubes	4	Shorting and poor emission
122	6SN7 Tube	2	Poor emission
118	6AC7 Tube	1	Shorting
127	705A Tube	3	Not known
116	505G Tube	5	Shorting & poor emission
129	717A Tube	2	Soft
119	6H6 (glass) Tube	1	Shorted
114	2X2 Tube	1	Gasious
135A	5D21 Tube	1	Shorted

133	836 Tube	1	Not known & one accidentally broken
128	7D6AY (Magnatron)	2	Low R.F.
97	Voltmeter 0-50 volts	1	Shorted out
104	Renewal links for 6 amp fuses	32	Overload
106	Renewal links for 10 amp fuses	18	Overload
213	Capacitor, mica 240 mf 500 volts	1	Not within tolerance
236	Cable assembly, coaxial	1	Arcing
242	Modulation Network	3	Leaking oil
281	Resistor, .18 megs 1/2 watt	1	Open
349	Resistor, .15 meg 2 watt	1	Burned out
350	Resistor, 1 meg 2 watts	1	Not within tolerance
361	Resistor, 100 ohms 2 watts	1	added to set
366	Resistor, 10,000 ohms wire wound	1	Open
363	Resistor, 1,600 ohms wire wound	1	Burned out
411	Resistor, 10,000 ohms 2 watts	1	Below tolerance rating
444	Resistor, 7 megs 10 watts	1	Not within tolerance
342	Resistor, 2,200 ohms 2 watts	1	Burned out
410	Resistor, 10,000 ohms 2 watts	1	Open
185	Capacitor, .5 mf 600 volts	1	Leakage
148	Capacitor, .1/.1 mf 600 volts	1	Leakage

SJ-1 N.G.

19	Resistor, [IPR] Designation 589540́5AB1	1	Open
20	Resistor, [IPR] Designation 589540́5AB2	1	Damaged in repairing
25	Brushes, ([?]" Axis) [RFR] Designation 810993AA4	1	Worn out
27	Rotating Elements, NTR Designation 8109978AC1	1	Worn out

(N) SOUND GEAR AND SOUND CONDITIONS

Normal.

(O) DENSITY LAYERS

None observed that have not been previously reported by other submarines.

(P) HEALTH, FOOD, & HABITABILITY

Good.

(R) PERSONNEL

(a)	Men on board during patrol	72
(b)	Men qualified at start of patrol	24
(c)	Men qualified at end of patrol	59
(d)	Men unqualified making first patrol	6
(e)	Men advanced in rating	18

(R) MILES STEAMED - FUEL USED

Base to Area	Miles	Gallons
Enroute Palau	3,500	27,000
Enroute Davao and return	900	4,000
Enroute Truk	1,050	8,500
	5,450	39,500

On Station	2,600	27,000
Enroute Pearl	3,100	30,000
	11,150	96,500

(S) DURATION

Days enroute Palau	11
Days enroute Davao	1½
Days returning Palau	3
Days returning Truk	5½
Days in areas	29
Days enroute Pearl	10
	60
Days submerged	24

(T) FACTORS OF ENDURANCE REMAINING

Torpedoes	Fuel	Provisions	Personnel Factor
24	2,000	15 days	Unlimited

(U) REMARKS

Identification:

The twenty-two aviators who witnessed a demonstration of submarine identification flares Mk 10, 11, and 12, submarine emergency identification signals Mk 2 Mod 2 (ex-smoke bombs), and Mk 1 comets (Buck Rogers gun), unanimously doubt their ability to note any but the Mk 1 comet, and that one, too, if already diving for an attack. Along this same line is the fact that every pyrotechnic we could fire did not deter a friendly submarine from making an end around on us during our last patrol, forcing us to avoid at high speed as soon as he dived. Sure identification is becoming increasingly important as we traverse a thousand extra miles of U.S. patrolled waters. Further, it may not always be possible or desireable to establish sanctuaries in coming operations, such an incident arising in this very patrol when an enemy submarine shared our area for a day or more.

Means for realistic identification is at hand in the simple Mk 3 (mortar type) signal projector, which was issued to submarines during 1938, but ordered turned in before many were installed. The order to turn them in was based on the fact that the submarine signal gun could fire pyrotechnics of similar color. The person issuing the order evidently did not consider the prohibitive delay in the use of the submerged signal gun for a surface projector. The Mk 3 projector mentioned above provides a healthy pyrotechnic were it can be seen in a matter of a second or two, and its effectiveness was demonstrated in one of our submarines who reinstalled one prior to returning to the coast after her first patrol. It successfully warded off numerous Army planes, certainly the crucial test. It is our present intention to procure one, at least for demonstration during the training period.

The fact that one of the pilots later recovered observed our green Very stars during our night screen east of Truk but was afraid to answer, indicated the need for a simple identification under those circumstances. Rather than reverting to any complicated arrangement using a two or three color cartridge, especially as there is no advantage in having the submarine signal visible at a greater range than that from the raft, the following procedure is suggested as standard. If accepted and publicized among aviators, it could well facilitate some rescues:

(a) Submarine fire single green stars during night search as conditions permit.

(b) Raft reply with one of the five or six red stars with which each is now provided.

(c) Submarine on sighting red star immediately reply with two green stars and close the bearing, firing additional stars as necessary.

Night Periscope:

In agreement with the U.S.S. *Seahorse,* it is hoped that the night periscope is not being held up by design difficulties of the radar feature. The periscope itself will eliminate that "between the dark and the moonlight" period when proper attack is near impossible. This is nine tenths of what is desired. Though the radar feature is very desirable, the ability to see the target group at considerable range will permit an aggressive submerged approach with firing ranges that will insure the hits.

Submarine Radar:

It was most disappointing to learn that the proposed aircraft search radar had been abandoned in favor of improvements to the present SD. The size of the "bed spring" and the 60 degree overhead void were evidently the main objection.

The objection by commanding officers to the moderate size antenna is inconsistent, for there is hardly a submarine whose shears do not bulge with underwater loops, CUO antennas, lookout platforms, binocular rests, and "clear the bridge" poles. Further, the proposed antenna could doubtless be designed to fold automatically in the manner of a music stand.

The sixty degree blank cone overhead, which at first appeared frightening, could well be given a little more thought. Personal conversation with Commander Bernstein last summer indicated that this radar would be infallible in detecting planes up to twelve miles. In other words, unless the enemy were coming from Mars, he would have to be flying at approximately 50,000 feet to escape detection. Except in radar equipped planes, airmen admit that they'll probably not spot a submarine when flying above 15,000 feet, and will surely not detect him under the best conditions when above 25,000 feet. Thus the proposed radar seems to offer a substantial safety factor.

Overlooking the above, the weakness of the present SD is not in its very few internal failures, but in its unpredictable voids, its inability to detect low flying planes, and the obvious ease with which the enemy is DF'ing and perhaps homing on it.

Granting that any radar equipment must be accepted with its limitations, the enemy is not standing still, and the limitations of the SD may before long preclude its general use. A static program of only improving present equipment is therefore unsound and should be avoided. A farsighted program would include addition of the proposed aircraft search radar, with improvements to the present SD. If below deck space is a problem in this installation, there's a ship's office any boat would donate. If it is topside space, a permanent feeder running inside or outside the conning tower, thence between periscope shears to fixed SD radiators at shear top level would leave the after space available for a "bed spring" aircraft search radar.

Except for internal failures, which will undoubtedly be ironed out by installation of more substantial parts, the SJ at present is a near ideal search and attack radar. We are, however, accepting a reduced range simply because of the relatively low height of the reflector compared to the much similar SG installations in surface craft. In addition to the greater area that could be covered with a higher reflector, is the probable necessity of tracking the enemy at greater ranges as his radar improves. The design problems of a raisable reflector are not insurmountable. One could and should be designed to operate at both the present shear top level and in a raised position at the height of our raised periscopes. The most logical way to accomplish this would be the new aircraft detection radar in the place now occupied by the SD mast. By removing the SD housing pipe, in the conning tower, and installing a well, the present hoist could raise this unit to the desired level. A clutch type coupling, similar to our original periscope bearing transmitter coupling, would provide a ready means for power rotation of the mast in its raised or lowered positions. The wave guide could be telescopic, with transmitter output fed to it near the bottom of the well. If the present reflector is too heavy, a metal sprayed plastic one could be substituted.

The minimum we should now be striving for is then a two position SJ, an airplane search radar to augment the SD, and the coming periscope radar.

Though the above opinions and ideas may seem too futuristic, it must be remembered again that the enemy is not sitting still. We are still enjoying, though on the waining edge, an immense tactical advantage over him because of speed and radar. However the minute we say "this is good enough," we're losing the offensive and he is catching up. It will then be just a matter of time until submarines are again the "submerged vessels of opportunity" we used to believe them to be.

Submarine Division Forty-Four

FB5-44/A16-3   Care of Fleet Post Office
                                               San Francisco, California
Serial: (039)   21 May 1944.

C-O-N-F-I-D-E-N-T-I-A-L

First Endorsement to
USS *Tang* Second War
Patrol Report.

From:		The Commander Submarine Division Forty-Four.
To:		The Commander-in-Chief, U.S. Fleet.
Via:	(1)	The Commander Submarine Squadron Four.
	(2)	The Commander Submarine Force, Pacific Fleet
	(3)	The Commander-in-Chief, U.S. Pacific Fleet.

Subject: U.S.S. *Tang* Second War Patrol – Comments on.

1.   Although disappointing in that no shipping loss was incurred by the enemy, the second war patrol of the *Tang* under Lieutenant Commander R.H. O'Kane as commanding officer was equally as outstanding as his first. By virtue

of remarkable cooperation with aircraft of the U.S. striking force attacking Truk, willingness to proceed from point to point within gun range of shore batteries in order to rescue expeditiously personnel of downed aircraft, and seizing the initiative by bombarding known gun emplacements when passing Ollan Island, twenty-two U.S. naval aviation personnel were rescued from lifeboats and downed aircraft. During the sixty day patrol, twenty-nine days were spent on assigned stations in Palau, Davao and Truk areas. No doubt the scarcity of targets is attributable in part to the presence of a heavy U.S. task force in the western Pacific.

2. Of five surface craft contacts, three were small patrol craft and evaded, one was an [*sic*] RO class submarine which dived at a range of 3,000 yards on appearance of U.S. aircraft, and one smoke contact on two ships. It was impossible to close this contact because of combination of air screen attacks proximity to shoal water on Grey Feather Bank and operation order to take a lifeguard station. Of fifty aircraft contacts, twenty-two were sighted by periscope, eight were observed first by radar while four were made jointly by radar and sight, fifteen were seen by bridge personnel during daylight and one was discovered at night due to carrying running lights.

3. The performance of the SJ radar can not be classed as completely satisfactory due to the excessive time under repair and the abnormal quantity of spares required for maintenance. The comments of the commanding officer on the general subject of radar are well taken; the use of both SD and SJ radar must be supervised carefully to prevent aiding the enemy in counter measures. Until such time as radar equipment not susceptible of enemy detection is available again to submarines, it will be necessary to utilize other equipment, primarily sound gear, to obtain data provided previously by radar. Periscope radar is required now more than a year ago.

4. With the number of submarines being used on lifeguard stations and the morale effect on aviators participating in such raids, it is felt that a certain means of ready identification between submarines and the aviation personnel is essential. Good voice communications between planes and submarines is required. Air coverage of lifeguard submarines permits freedom of action by the submarine in moving from point to point in effecting rescues.

5. Health and morale of *Tang* personnel was excellent. It is noteworthy that thirty-five men were qualified in submarines during this patrol, while eighteen out of a total of seventy-two on board were advanced in rating. The *Tang* will undergo normal refit by Submarine Base, Pearl Harbor with particular attention being paid to radar equipment, and conversion of number four main ballast tank into fuel ballast tank.

6. The commanding officer, officers and crew are congratulated on the rescue of twenty-two officers and men of the naval aviation service.

E. R. Swinburne,
Acting.

Submarine Squadron Four   11/jet

FC5-4/A16-3   Fleet Post Office,
                                              San Francisco, Calif.

Serial 0195

CONFIDENTIAL

Second Endorsement to
U.S.S. *Tang* Second War
Patrol Report.

From: The Commander Submarine Squadron Four
To: The Commander-in-Chief, United States Fleet
Via: (1) The Commander Submarine Force, Pacific Fleet
           (2) the Commander-in-Chief, U.S. Pacific Fleet

Subject: U.S.S. *Tang* Second War Patrol – comments on.

1.   Forwarded, concurring in the remarks of Comander Submarine Division Forty-Four.
2.   The lifeguard methods employed by the Commanding Officer, U.S.S. *Tang*, coupled with his remarks on this type of operation have been made a basis for training potential "life-guards."
3.   Commander Submarine Squadron Four adds his congratulations to those of the entire service for the outstanding seamanship, tenacity and courage displayed by the Commanding Officer, officers and crew of the U.S.S. *Tang*.

C.B. Momsen

Submarine Force, Pacific Fleet   heh
FF12-10/A16-3(15)/(16)

Serial 01028

Care of Fleet Post Office,
San Francisco, California,
27 May 1944.

CONFIDENTIAL

Third Endorsement to
Tang Report of
Second War Patrol.

Note: This report will be
destroyed prior to
entering patrol area.

ComSubPac Patrol Report No. 426.
U.S.S. *Tang* – Second War Patrol.

From: The Commander Submarine Force, Pacific Fleet.
To: The Commander-in-Chief, United States Fleet.
Via: The Commander-in-Chief, U.S. Pacific Fleet.

Subject: U.S.S. *Tang* (SS306) – Report of Second war Patrol.
(16 March to 15 May 1944).

1.   The *Tang*'s second war patrol was conducted in areas northwest of Palau, west of Davao, and in the vicinity of Truk.

2.   This entire patrol was outstanding in patrol efficiency, excellent initiative, and aggressive spirit. Throughout the patrol the *Tang* used all of its equipment to the utmost efficiency.

3.   The remarkable recovery of 22 Naval aviators in seven different pickups close to the reef at Truk and within enemy gun range is a sterling example of how cooperation between the submarine performing lifeguard duty and the planes of the striking air forces can, by cooperation, make successful recoveries of our down aviators. The aggressive, successful, and well planned bombardment of Ollan Island contributed much to the eventual rescue of the downed aviators. This patrol report should be carefully studied by all Commanding Officers as a guide for future lifeguard duty.

4.   It is of note that the *Tang*'s contact with the *Trigger* and subsequent exchange of necessary spare parts was instrumental in the latter vessel continuing on a patrol that inflicted severe damage to the enemy.

5.   The remarks made by the Commanding Officer regarding the present and future uses of radar by submarines are greatly appreciated. The Pro-Sub

sections in this area and in the Department are constantly working on all new developments, including radar.

    6.   This patrol is designated as successful for Combat Insignia Award.

    7.   The Commander Submarine Force, Pacific Fleet, congratulates the Commanding Officer, officers, and crew for the aggressive and efficient manner in which the lifeguard duty was performed resulting in the recovery of 22 Naval aviators.

C.A. Lockwood, Jr.

DISTRIBUTION:
(Complete Reports)

Cominch	(7)
CNO	(5)
CinCpac	(6)
Intel.Cen.Pac.Ocean Areas	(1)
ComServPac	
(Adv. Base Plan Unit)	(1)
CinClant	(2)
ComSubLant	(8)
S/M School, NL	(2)
ComSoPac	(2)
ComSoWesPac	(1)
ComSubsoWestPac	(2)
CTF 72	(2)
ComNorPac	(1)
ComSubsPac	(40)
SUBAD, MI	(2)
ComSubsPacSubOrdCon	(3)
All Squadron and Div.	
Commanders, SubsPac	(2)
ComSubsTrainPac	(2)
All Submarines, SubsPac	(1)

E.L. Hymes, 2nd.
Flag Secretary.

Patrol Three, 8 June 1944 – 14 July 1944

U.S.S. *Tang* (SS 306)
c/o Fleet Post Office,
San Francisco, Calif.

A16-3
Serial 011
CONFIDENTIAL

July 14, 1944.

From: The Commanding Officer.
To: The Commander in Chief, United States Fleet.
Via: The Commander Submarine Division 141.
           The Commander Submarine Squadron 14.
           The Commander Submarine Force, Pacific Fleet.
           The Commander in Chief, U.S. Pacific Fleet.

Subject: U.S.S. *Tang* (SS 306), Report of Third War Patrol.

Enclosures: (A) Subject Report.
              (B) Track Chart (Comsubpac only.)

1. Enclosure (a), covering the third war patrol of this vessel conducted in the East China and the Yellow Sea during the period 8 June 1944 to 14 July 1944, is forwarded herewith.

R.H. O'Kane

(A) PROLOGUE

Returned from second war patrol May fifteenth and completed normal refit on the thirtieth. Conducted port repair trials, training with three days underway, loaded, and departed June 8.

(B) NARRATIVE

June 8 – 12

1330 Underway in company with U.S.S. *Sealion* for Midway, conducting training dives, fire control drills, and testing communications for future coordinated patrol.

June 12 (-12)

0800 Arrived Midway, fueled, and located motor ground in a brush pigtail. Held dock trial to insure that trouble had been remedied.

1600 Departed for East China Sea at two engine speed.

June 12 (-12) – 21(-9)

Enroute area, delaying an hour near Sofu Gan to tune SJ radar. As experience in training showed that we could clear seven lookouts and the OOD from the bridge without delaying the dive, used this number in the daytime and kept the SD secured. We sighted no planes and none apparently sighted us.

June 22 (-9)

1706 Dived thirty miles from Yaku Shima prior to pass through Colonet Strait after dark.

2000 Shortly after surfacing picked up 142 megacycle radar, apparently on Yaku Shima, with our APR-1 equipment, so gave it a wide berth, using our SJ periodically and never within forty-five degrees of the island. Though this is an arbitrary safety angle, an island that has radar will most certainly have detectors, too, and the least one can expect is re-routed shipping.

June 23 (-9)

0350 Made rendezvous with *Sealion* south of Kusakaki Shima, a little late as we had delayed to investigate a possible SJ contact. Patrolled submerged southwest of the island during the day, but with periodic high periscope searches.

2000 Proceeded to Danjo Gunto to meet U.S.S. *Tinosa*.

June 24 – 25

0115 Made scheduled rendezvous with *Tinosa* and *Sealion* fifteen miles south of Danjo Gunto. Executive Officer went aboard *Tinosa*, delivering infra-red signalling apparatus, code for coordinated attacks, and *Tang's* ideas for patrolling this area. With everything in agreement, proceeded northeast for submerged patrol south of Fukue Shima, prior to closing Koshiki Straits.

0808 Sighted small patrol boat and avoided submerged.

2145 After dodging numerous lighted sampans along the 100 fathom curve, sighted a large convoy on the SJ at 20,000 yards, just having emerged from Koshiki Straits.

2153 As course and speed were at first ambiguous, sent contact report of convoy's position only. *Sealion* acknowledged.

2220 Having tracked convoy on course between 315 and 270 at speeds from 10 to 16 knots, answered *Tinosa's* request for convoy course and speed.

2227 Sent latest course of 230 and speed 12.

We were in what at first appeared a fortunate position on the convoy's port bow, with a three day old moon about to set, but as numerous bow and flanking escorts appeared on the radar screen it seemed evident that undetected penetration from ahead or from the flank would be nearly impossible.

The composition of the convoy, which had been confused by numerous escorts and side lobes, now was clarified with visual sighting. There were at least six large ships, in column sections of two, surrounded by two circular screens of at least six escorts each, and as we later discovered, each section was further escorted ahead and astern.

Attacks No's 1 and 2

As the quarter escorts were well dispersed, elected to approach from the stern. We passed between them without difficulty, diverged to starboard and avoided a third patrol and gained position 2,500 yards on the starboard beam of the last section.

The leading ship was a large modern four mast or goalpost freighter with high composite superstructure topped by a large short stack, believed to be (EU)[1] of the *Aobasan Maru* class, page 84, ONI 208-J (rev'd). The second ship was a modern tanker with large short funnel, similar (EU) to the *Genyo Maru* or *Kyokuto Maru*, page 277 or 279, ONI 208-J (rev'd). Both ships were heavily loaded, and most probably diesel driven as they did not smoke.

---

[1] (EU): Estimate Unconfirmed. A positive identification of a ship or ship class is noted as (EC), or Estimate Confirmed. The usual reference source for merchant shipping was *ONI 208-J: Japanese Merchant Ships: Recognition Manual.* The "EU" notation became more common as the war progressed and the Japanese built new classes of merchant vessels.

2349 The convoy, now close to Nomo Saki, had settled on course north at 10 knots when we stopped, turned left for straight

2352 shot, and fired three torpedoes at the freighter, 120 starboard track, range 2,600, spread his length by constant

2353 TBT bearings, followed immediately by a similar spread at the tanker, 100 starboard track, range 2,450. All gyros were between 12 right and 2 left. Observed two beautiful hits in the stern and amidships of the freighter, timed as our first and third torpedoes. The second was observed to run erratically to the left. The explosions appeared to blow the ship's sides out, and he commenced sinking rapidly. On schedule, our fourth and fifth torpedoes hit under the stack and just forward of the after superstructure of the tanker. His whole after end blazed up until extinguished as he went down by the stern.

0000 We had now evaded the closest escort at 1,400 yards apparently unobserved, so pulled up seven thousand yards from the convoy and five thousand yards from where our targets would have been. Their pips, separating from the convoy, had gradually disappeared from the PPI screen however, and only a low hanging cloud of smoke marked the spot where they sank.

0015 Sent message to other boats that we were trailing and gave convoy's set-up, and repeated it twenty minutes later at *Sealion*'s request.

0020 As the only radar interference indicated that our other boats would not get in, especially as the convoy was close to Nagasaki, whose steel mills loomed up like Marin Ship, started in for another attack. Our approach was spurred by an escort who closed in to fifteen hundred yards as we passed the vicinity of the first attack, but unable to see us in the haze of a slight overload, commenced dropping terrific depth charges. He succeeded in calling out the dogs however, and our target, which was first tracked at ten knots, showed stopped, then a range rate of better than forty knots closing! He had just time to complete a 90 degree turn when he passed sixteen hundred yards astern, a modern looking DE. He spotted us, closed for a minute, but our team of overload experts, watching their temperatures, got us rolling at 22½ knots in spite of our unconverted #4 MBT. Easing off each time he showed a slight angle, we opened the range to 3,400 yards when he illuminated. Hoping to take advantage of the experience of others, we dived a little faster than a rock, encouraged by a sounding taken during the chase. Though his searchlight illuminated the bridge diving alarm for our PCO[2], he still did not spot us, and passed well clear, madly echo ranging.

0200 Now with the time to consider, believed the Nagasaki area would be

[2] PCO: Prospective Commanding Officer. An officer making a war patrol as an observer before being assigned as CO of his own submarine. In this case, Lieutenant Commander Morton H. Lytle, who would later command U.S.S. *Burrfish* (SS-312) on two war patrols.

very unhealthy at dawn two hours hence, so surfaced and rounded the Koshiki Islands where we could guard the southern approaches to the straits.

0500 Commenced submerged patrol.

1900 Sighted patrol boat on northerly course; avoided.

June 26 (-9)
Attack Number 3

0424 Shortly after crack of dawn sighted ship on the SJ at 8,000 yards which had just rounded Noma Saki from the Koshiki Straits. We were already on his beam, but fog and rain permitted a full power end-around with only occasional glimpses of our enemy. He was a medium sized, split superstructure, MFM freighter, similar (EU) to the *Erimo Maru*, page 228, ONI 208-J (rev'd), tracked at eight knots on courses hugging the coast. With the freighter obscured by rain, dived a thousand yards off his track, range 7,000 yards. As we were 3,000 yards west of Bono Misaki, a good firing range was insured. Turned right for

0551 a stern shot as the freighter came out of the rain and fired four Mk 18 torpedoes, range 1,950, 100 starboard track, gyros near 180, spread his length by constant bearings. The torpedoes were set on six feet as the sea was calm and the loading of the freighter could not be ascertained beforehand. Though we had a zero angle on the boat, two of the torpedoes broached several times and then settled down on surface runs, throwing continuous plumes in the air. Needless to say the freighter avoided the spread by turning toward. All exploders operated as the torpedoes hit the beach if that is any consolation. After some gunfire, the freighter took refuge in a cove north of Bono Misaki, and as we were getting set toward

0640 the beach, surfaced and made a full power dash to the west, unsighted by a late arriving patrol boat.

June 27 (-9)

0958 Dived when overcast lifted.

1008 Sighted "Betty" searching.

1608 Sighted "Betty" searching again.

1758 Sighted "Dave" searching.

2000 Proceeded to the northwest for coordinated patrol with *Tinosa* and *Sealion* of a suspected Shimonoseki–Shanghai traffic route. Passed numerous lighted sampans.

June 28 (-9)

Conducted submerged high periscope patrol on direct route between Shimonoseki and Shanghai.

1945 Continued to the northwest at one engine speed.

2000 Detected 150 megacycle radar on either Saishu To[3] or Mara To, so rounded them at fifteen miles to avoid possibility of detection and followed our usual policy of not training the SJ within 45 degrees of known radar installations except for a fast periodic sweep.

June 29 (-9)

0220 When 40 miles northwest of Saishu To, detected weak 95 megacycle radar, perhaps from eastern end of that island, and at the same time commenced tracking a radar contact near Kakyo To at 26,000 yards. This proved to be side lobes of the island. The strength of our 95 megacycle radar did not increase as we approached Kakyo To, so this island is eliminated as a possible source.

0441 Commenced submerged patrol near Hen Sho, half way between Kakyo To and Santai To off the southwest coast of Korea.

This position was close to the suspected route across the Yellow Sea to the China coast. Low fast moving fog patches and fogging periscopes made searching difficult, so came to radar depth periodically.

Attack No's. 4A and 4B.

1140 Sighted a freighter to the north on a westerly course. Commenced approach, but it soon became apparent that we could not reach an attack position submerged. We therefore opened the range on a diverging course, surfaced, and commenced an "end around" bucking a heavy sea. Reduced visibility permitted passing the ship with only occasional glimpses at 15,000 yards.

1600 Having tracked the enemy on course 255 at 7 knots, dived directly on his track for periscope attack. The freighter came on nicely, identified (EC) as the *Tazan Maru*, page 215 ONI 208-J (rev'd). His masts had been cut off level with the top of his stack, but all other details were as shown. He was lightly loaded, but in view of our experience of the twenty-seventh, decided that ten feet was the absolute minimum depth setting for this one.

After two "dipsy doodles[4]" to adjust position, and several echo ranges and

1759 bearings checking, fired two Mk 14 torpedoes, one at his foremast and one at his mainmast, 90 port track, range 1,250 yeard, speed seven. Raised the periscope again to see the smoke of each torpedo at its point of aim, but they apparently passed under.

The enemy turned toward and gave us two close depth charges shortly after we had reached two hundred feet, fifty feet off the bottom. Fifteen minutes

---

[3] Saishu To: Also known as Quelpart Island.

[4] Dipsy Doodle: A maneuver in which the submarine makes a gradual turn off the target's track, then a sharp turn back toward the track, so that the bow tubes are lined up properly for a shot. The path on a chart would look something like a question mark.

later, as we were approaching periscope depth, a loud crackling noise came over sound followed by a third fairly close charge.

1910 We went back down, but searched and surfaced fifteen minutes later with nothing in sight. This points to the possibility that this last was a delayed action depth charge used in the shallow water for the purpose of keeping a submarine down while the ship escapes.

2030 It didn't work in this case, however, for we made radar contact in a little over an hour and commenced tracking again. Our enemy had gone to the north, was tracked on course 040, then 070 at ten knots, heading for Ko To and the ten fathom curve off the Korea coast. We closed sufficiently to identify him, and then turned the tracking over to the section on watch with the plan to attack after sunset in the lee of Daikokusan Gunto.

June 30 (-9)

The freighter was a little out in his navigation, however, his track passing about fifteen miles north of the island. As firing in the lee was now impossible and the sea rougher still, determined to attack from a range to insure hits even with broaching torpedoes.

0040 Commenced approach from his starboard bow directly down wind and sea, stopped with range 1,500, angle on the bow

1010 40 starboard, killed headway as he came on, and fired a Mk 14 "feeler" torpedo set on six feet from number five tube, range 750 yards, 92 starboard track, 6 degree left gyro, enemy speed nine knots. In spite of the heavy seas it ran perfectly, its phosphorescent track visible among the white caps right to the freighter's side. The explosion amidships, just thirty seconds after firing, was as beautiful as it was reassuring.

It broke the freighter's back, his stern sinking with a down angle, his forward section with an up, in a cloud of fire, smoke, and steam.

His gun crew had guts, however, and got off five or six shots in spite of their tilting platform. When they had ceased firing we relieved about twenty lookouts in rapid succession, and today our crew is discussing singe versus multiple torpedo fire. (We'll continue, however, to fire as many as is considered necessary to sink the enemy.)

The inability of the enemy to sight us is considered due in part to our light gray camouflage, local for this area, and the known inefficiency of lookout into wind and sea.

0130 Proceeded to the west for submerged patrol after daylight.

July 1 (-8)

Commenced submerged patrol one hour after dawn, forty miles

0946 west of Ko To. Maneuvered to close a sailing junk, and surfaced to look him over. He lowered his sails after four rounds of four inch, but our plan to get some information from him became unnecessary when our high lookout sighted smoke over the horizon.

Attack Number 5

1015 Commenced tracking smoke which quickly developed into two columns, and then the masts of two ships. One ship was zigging at intervals of from three to twelve minutes, while the other's movements indicated an escort. After gaining position ahead and tracking these ships on base course 260

1322 at eight knots, dived for periscope approach and attack. As the group came on, maneuvered for a Mk 18 stern shot at the escort who was about 1,500 yards on the freighter's starboard bow. This placed us directly ahead of the freighter and insured a stern shot at him if the escort was not hit. The escort was now identified as a small engines aft freighter with gun forward and depth charges aft, probably the 1940 series (EU) of the *Amakasu Maru*, page 270, ONI 208-J (rev'd), changed in that the bridge structure was aft. As TDC bearings were lagging, took several echo ranges and found his speed had

1444 increased to ten knots. Now with the set-up checking, fired two Mk 18 torpedoes, one under his foremast, the other under his stack, 100 port track, range 1,250, depth setting six feet, then went ahead at standard speed to gain position on the freighter.

As the moments dragged out the time for the torpedoes to hit had apparently passed, expressed some quiet oaths about electric torpedoes, only to have the words jammed down our throats by a swell explosion. Slowed and looked to see the escort's stern in the air in a cloud of smoke, and freighter turning back. At least half a dozen persons observed this ship sink, timed in two minutes and twenty seconds.

Attack Number 6

We now felt that we had the freighter caught between third base and home, for he was nearly one hundred miles from the Korean coast and his track led through the probable positions of both *Sealion* and *Tinosa*. Sent them the contact report on the next hourly schedule and continued trailing submerged at five knots. With the smoke still in sight.

1916 surfaced at dusk and commenced overtaking at full power on three engines, charging with the other and the auxiliary. Again we're thankful for our Fairbanks-Morse, for as it later proved, our eighteen and a half knots in this combination was every bit necessary.

After radar contact with the enemy had been gained it became apparent that we would have to pass him up when south of Ko To, but with full power on two main engines, we were waiting for him with two minutes to spare as he approached the southern tip of the island.

2224 Dived a mile and half off the island, 1,200 yards north of the track of the convoy who was now six thousand yards away. He slowed from eleven to nine knots as he passed southern tip, but with three echo ranges and periscope bearings, the set-up was checking again as we commenced our turn for a straight bow shot. With range 500, 90 port track,

2247 gyros near zero, fired two Mk 14 torpedoes by constant bearings, the first at the middle of his after well deck, the second at the middle of his forward one. The first torpedo hit as aimed in twenty seconds, exploding the ship's cargo, which must have been munitions of some sort. A short section of the bow was all that remained intact of the whole ship, and it sunk in twenty seconds. The second torpedo was "robbed."

This was a medium freighter, identified during and after attack number 5 and at close range by moonlight prior to firing as similar (EU) to the *Samarang Maru*, page 130, ONI 208-J (rev'd).

2251 Surfaced close to debris and proceeded sixty miles to west for our usual patrol.

July 2 (-8)
Conducted submerged patrol with high periscope searches.
1007 Sighted masts of two trawlers.

July 3 (-8)
Patrolled as day before.
2250 Made scheduled rendezvous with *Sealion*, and executive officer boarded her to exchange information. She was unable to reach our first convoy, and failed to receive our message concerning the freighter, but had sunk an AK on the way to this expected traffic route. It will be interesting to compare the reports of *Sealion* and *Tinosa* with ours, for the expected route runs between their area as assigned by *Tinosa*[5], while ours lies to the north. They have in general patrolled on the surface using their SD and have been driven down by planes. Though this may not be conclusive, it appears that they have shunted the traffic by us, for we've been patrolling submerged, surfacing for a good look now and then, and keeping SD secured. We've seen ships and no planes since after our attack on the 27th.

The Sealion has decided to patrol the Shanghai area, while we proceed north.

[5] "as assigned by *Tinosa*...": Having graduated from the United States Naval Academy in 1929, *Tinosa*'s commanding officer, Donald F. Weiss was senior to both O'Kane, 1934, and Eli T. Reich, 1935, *Sealion*'s CO. As senior officer Weiss was the one who assigned the individual patrol areas within the larger area assigned to the three submarines.

July 4 (-8) (What a Fourth!)

0005 Set course for position on the direct route between Daikokusan Gunto and Osei To at three engine speed. As the sky was overcast at dawn, continued on the surface, and shortly

0405 sighted heavy masts of a ship to the northeast.

Attack Number 7

Stopped, put him astern, and determined his approximate northerly course, and commenced a full power dash to get on his track. We were a bit hampered by fifteen trawlers or fishermen, but with the enemy's bridge and stack aft already over the horizon, it was their presence which prevented our detection.

0500 With angle on the bow now 5 starboard, dived and continued approach. The massiveness of the ship as it closed resembled a man-of-war, and twenty minutes later a wide zig gave us our first good identification look. Her hull and arrangement were similar (EU) to the *Kurosio Maru*, page 272, ONI 208-J (rev'd), with modifications as shown in accompanying drawing.

During the next hour we were abaft his beam as he closed the ten fathom curve, zigging leisurely. On our straight course at full speed we closed the range continuously however, and though on most observations with angles on the bow up to 150 the situation looked hopeless, he finally reached a nine fathom finger west of Amma To and came back to a southerly course. Our fathometer, which had been showing four fathoms under our keep, now in quick succession showed three, two, and then merged with the outgoing signal,

0626 so we backed down and fired three Mk 14 torpedoes at stack, amidships, and forward by constant bearings, range 2,600, 90 starboard track, speed 8, depth setting eight feet. Turned left with full speed and rudder, and heard healthy hits timed as our first and second torpedoes. We slowed and looked to see only the bow, stern, and masts sticking out of the water under a huge cloud of smoke.

0631 Surfaced, surrounded by 34 assorted fishing boat obviously awe-stricken. There were about fifty survivors in the water and large life boats, but as we could not dive in the eight to nine fathoms if we approached closer, headed west at three engine speed. The stern had sunk before we surfaced, and as we cleared the area, observed the protruding bow tip go under in bubbling foaming water.

This ship was observed at moderate ranges from various angles for over an hour, and the following features indicate that she was for use as an (XAV) seaplane tender or aircraft transport; Her masts and booms were approximately twice as heavy as those of a large freighter. Her bridge structure was open aft forming a hanger. Her stern had been extended by a large platform with triangular stern piece and was fitted with kingposts and long boom. An auxiliary radio mast topped her after superstructure, fitted with several antennas. The survivors were far in excess of a normal tanker crew. Except for her black stack and masts, she was war color.

Comparing this ship with similar conversions in available publications, her standard displacement is estimated at sixteen thousand.

0730 When well clear of any small craft which could report our course, headed north and dived an hour and a half later, forty miles from the position of our attack.

1150 Commenced hearing very distant explosions, probably 52 miles distant to be exact.

1840 Having passed Osei To, sighted smoke beyond the Onyo group of Islands, tracked on a southerly course. While figuring where and how we could get him under a full moon in more than then fathoms, our problem was solved by a faint wisp of smoke to the west.

Attack Number 8

Switched approach to this, and closed at standard speed submerged until clear of Osei To, then surfaced in

1953 late twilight, but under a full moon. Twenty minutes later he was sighted on the radar at 18,500 yards. We were in a fortunate position ahead and had only to move on to his course of 110, which lead toward Osei To and the bulge of the ten fathom curve. His long low silhouette was visible at 15,000 yards, so tracked from that range, determining his moderate zigs of 20 to 30 degrees at 5 to 10 minute intervals.

2041 Dived and tracked enemy in by radar to 9,000 yards, then commenced moonlight periscope attack.

As we came on his silhouette developed into a long engines aft ship with raked bow, and with tripod mast and king posts forward and aft. Distinctive also was his mushroom topped bridge structure. After closing a left zig at standard speed,

2122 checked set-up with several echo ranges, and first last two bow torpedoes, one at forward end of after superstructure, the other forward of his bridge, range 900 yards, 90 starboard track, gyros near zero, depth setting eight feet. The first torpedo hit just aft of the bridge, breaking the ship's back. The tripod foremast could be seen in the smoke and debris tilting aft as he sank by the middle. Let the crew

2131 hear the breaking up noises by the sound – 1MC method, then surfaced to pick up a survivor. It was necessary to snake one of the two large overturned lifeboats alongside with grapnels, and threaten with Tommy gun bursts to convince the one visible survivor to come on board. Recovering a life ring was much simpler.

Both the new life boats, life ring, and visual observation of the vessel before firing show this to have been a new ship. She does not appear in any identification book. Our PCO and executive officer both observed this ship together with the commanding officer prior to firing, and estimate her tonnage to be 10,000, the same as the modern tanker her hull was designed after. With some assistance from the prisoner, the silhouette of this ship has been drawn and is submitted.

Of interest is the prisoner's knowledge of the exact position where they were torpedoed, and apparent familiarity with the shipping routes.

Not so clear are his figures on tonnage, which range from 7,000 to 10,200, but he finally got across the idea that this latter figure was iron ore in her holds. Phonetically her name was *Ama-aoka Maru* of the Yamashita Kisen Kaisho.

2328 After commencing another approach on what proved to be a sailing junk, headed northwest at three engine speed to round Kakureppi Island and approach the Daisei group before dawn.

July 5 – 6 (-8)

0345 Dived for submerged patrol.

0845 Commenced hearing distant explosions, indicating that the opposition is still way behind us.

0917 Sighted distant smoke drawing to the south close to the Korean shore, south of the Daisei Islands. Although this was inaccessible in six fathoms of water, it practically assured an early attack against this coastal traffic off Chosen Kan.

1942 Proceeded on the surface to Chosen Kan (Choppeki Point).

Attack Number 9

2257 When 8 miles west of Choppeki Point, after having tracked one side lobe and investigated several second pulse echoes, sighted a ship on the SJ at 29,000 yards. Stopped and tracked it out to 32,000 on a northerly course at 9 knots, then commenced a gruelling end around. Under a full moon on a rippleless sea, the ship was visible at 20,000 yards, so to insure an unalerted enemy for our last two torpedoes, passed

0227 him outside of 15,000. When 30 miles from Gaichosan Retto (Blonde Group), stopped on his track seven miles ahead for a final speed and course check, then dived on a parallel course for the submerged attack. Checked the set-up by a radar observation at five thousand yards when the freighter was temporarily lost in the surface haze, and immediately experienced hopelessly fogging periscope. The set-up checked perfectly, however, showing us 500 yards off the track, so returned to 60 feet to wet the scopes. He was clear and big on the next observation, at 1,100 yards by echo range,

0320 so turned for the stern shot. Fired two Mk 18 torpedoes, one at his mainmast, one at his foremast, range 900 yards, 90 starboard track, gyros near 180, depth setting 6 feet. Both torpedoes hit exactly as aimed and there was only floating wreckage and broken lifeboats in sight when we surfaced two minutes later. The freighter was medium sized, mast funnel mast, composite superstructure, similar (EU) to the *Osaka Maru*, page 132, ONI 208-J (rev'd).

0325 As two pips at 16,000 yards were closing, perhaps belated escorts, and the sky already pink, commenced full power

0600 run to the south toward Shantung Promontory. Dived fifty miles from the attack and proceeded south at three knots.

1202 Counter attack, seventy miles distant, commenced.

1848 Surfaced a half hour before sunset and continued the seven hundred mile run out of the area.

July 7 (-8)

0427 Shortly after sunrise dived for a "Betty."

1230 Continued surface running.

1914 Shortly after sunset, dived a half hour for a distant plane, believed a "Betty."

2055 Picked up 250 megacycle radar, random training.

2155 When between Danjo Gunto and the southern mine field, sighted five equal sized pips on the SJ at 16,000 yards on our track ahead. We were at four engine speed, which in part accounts for a range of 12,000 yards before we got them astern. The night was lightly overcast with a near full moon breaking through, but nothing was sighted on a fairly sharp horizon at this range. As we conducted a reverse end-around to get on their quarter, tracked the group on course 310, nearly the reverse of our original course, then 340, then 060. Closed their quarter cautiously until blinker signal was sighted at 13,000 yards, but no blurbs against the horizon. Five legitimate jap ships would contain at least one smoker and would have been visible at a much greater range. Convinced that this was a "killer group," undoubtedly directed by our late plane, gave them a wide berth and continued toward area boundary.

July 8 (-9)

0500 Commenced submerged approach of southern islands prior to night passage.

1600 Proceeded on surface.

1940 Detected 250 megacycle radar.

2106 A minute after sighting Gaja Shima light, observed a searchlight over the horizon to the right of the islands, and seventeen minutes later picked up 153 megacycle radar with random training.

2145 153 megacycle radar signal steadied at maximum strength, apparently trained on us. As we were already between Gaja Shima and Taira Shima at four engine speed, continued through the Nakano Strait into a rising moon. The 153 megacycle radar remained steady with maximum signal as we passed Nakano Shima, indicating its location there. Five small vessels, two of them smoking, heading from north and south into the strait, may have been patrols. If so, they were a little late, and no difficulty was experienced in keeping their bearings drawing aft with *Tang* at full power.

2300 Set course east, but continued at four engine speed during the night.

July 9 (-9)

0839 Dived for a half hour and apparently avoided detection by a distant low flying plane.

1210 Sighted flare, and friendly submarine surfaced about 4,000 yards on our starboard quarter. For the benefit of his fire control party, our base course was 090, speed 17, following cam #1 of our zig clock, making 15.8 good along the track.

2200 Sent message to ComSubPac concerning results, and information concerning killer group and departure for other boats.

July 10 (-9)

1030 Dived for fifteen minutes to avoid detection by a transport plane on a southerly course.

July 14 (+12)

1200 Arrived Midway.

(C) WEATHER

Normal for all localities patrolled.

(D) TIDAL INFORMATION

No information not previously reported.

(E) NAVIGATIONAL AIDS

1.	Osei To	Normal characteristics
2.	Kakurefei Retto	Normal characteristics

3.	Shusei To	Normal characteristics
4.	Danjo Gunto	Normal characteristics, but lighted intermittently
5.	Gaja Shima	Normal characteristics
6.	Shino Koshini	Normal characteristics
7.	Mara To	Dimmed
8.	Ko To (Daikokuzan Gunto)	Normal characteristics

(F) SHIP CONTACTS

See page 19A. [p. 71]

(G) AIRCRAFT CONTACTS

See page 20. [p. 72]

(H) ATTACK DATA

See page 21. [p. 73]

(I) MINES

None contacted.

(J) ANTI SUBMARINE MEASURES AND EVASIVE TACTICS

Except for the first convoy only one escort was encountered. The Japs were obviously unprepared and several hours late in their searches and indiscriminate depth charging and bombing. Evasion consisted of clearing the vicinity of the attack at high speed on the surface.

(K) MAJOR DEFECTS AND DAMAGE

None.

(L) RADIO

Both reception and transmission were satisfactory.
Tests of the lower frequencies assigned submarines were conducted with the U.S.S. *Sealion* while enroute Midway.

The results were startling in that the lowest two frequencies would not carry beyond six thousand yards in daytime and eleven thousand yards at night even with maximum power. It was also found that with minimum power the range of 2204 KCs could be reduced to about twenty miles. The data recorded though incomplete will be submitted to the Force Communications Officer. It is felt that further tests should be conducted to determine the limiting range of various frequencies for specific power settings of the TBL transmitter, as these could be of considerable value in coordinated attack group operation. Further it appears that a frequency lying between 450 and 2204 is desirable. It might even be advantageous if this fell in a Japanese broadcast band.

(M) RADAR

SJ Radar
The SJ radar gave comparatively little trouble during this patrol. This may have been due in part to its intermittent use, generally at 10 minute intervals. The part failures are listed below:

Item Number	Description	Number of Failures	Reason for Failure
12	Crystal	1	Bad TR tubes
130	TR Tube	1	Lost Vacuum
434	R 43	1	Voltage Surge
444	R 44	1	Voltage Surge
435	R 46	1	Voltage Surge
328	R 47	1	Voltage Surge
159	C 1	1	Voltage Surge

SD Radar
The SD radar was not used during this patrol.

RADAR DETECTOR CONTACTS (APR-1)

Submarine Position	Date	Freq.	Rotation sweep rate	Pulse Rate	Probable Location
18 mi. S. of Yaku Shima	4-22-44	95	Rotating sweep rate	600	Yaku Shima
25 mi. S. of Danjo Gunto	6-23-44	118	On 10 sec. off 20 sec.	60	U.S.S. *Sealion*

25 mi. S. of Danjo Gunto	6-23-44	95	Random train	900	Danjo Gunto
25 mi. S. of Danjo Gunto	6-23-44	235	Random train	60	
25 mi. S. of Danjo Gunto	6-23-44	174	Random train	60	
15 mi. S. of Mono Saki	6-24-44	87	Steady on	900	
31°-57' N 129°-31' E	6-25-44	260	Very weak	7 or 800	
20 mi. W. of Saishu To	6-28-44	150	Continuous	900	Saishu To
40 mi. NW of Saishu To	6-29-44	95	Very weak	900	
92 mi. West of Ko To	7-1-44	249	Fairly strong	900	
60 mi. West of Ko To	7-2-44	55	Random train	900	
40 mi. West of Ko To	7-3-44	255	Random train	900	
40 mi. bearing 120°T from Kakureppi Retto	7-5-44	249		900	
35 mi. South of Saishu To	7-7-44	250		900	

(S) DURATION

Days enroute to Midway	4
Days enroute Midway to Area	9
Days in Area	16
Days enroute to Midway	7
	36
Days Submerged	13

(T) FACTORS OF ENDURANCE REMAINING

Torpedoes	Fuel	Provisions	Personnel Factor
0	23,000	30 days	Indefinite

(U) MK 18 TORPEDOES

The Tang carried Mk 18 torpedoes in the after torpedo room. We experienced no difficulties. Routine was normal following that appearing in other patrol reports. Exchanging of torpedoes from cradles to tubes was not found necessary, however.

Date	Time	Lat.	Long.	Course	Speed	How Cont	Range	Type	Remarks
Ship Contacts									
6-24-44	2140	32-06 N	129-48 E	320	10	Radar	19,000	Convoy	6 ships, 1 escort
6-27-44	0424	31-16 N	130-15 E	140-110	8	Radar	8,000	Medium AK	
6-29-44	1140	34-30 N	124-50 E	265	7	Periscope	8,000	Medium AK	
7-1-44	0946	34-37 N	124-36 E	250	9	Sight	20,000	Medium AK	Escort AK
7-4-44	0400-0700	35-35 N	125-51 E	100-110	7	Sight	20,000	AO	Probably XAV
7-4-44	1953	36-06 N	125-52 E	100-042	9.5	Smoke	25,000	Ore Ship	
7-5-44	2253	38-10 N	124-15 E	317	9	SJ	28,450	Medium AK	
Small Craft									
6-24-44	0808	32-04 N	128-50 E	190		Periscope	6,000	Small fishing	
6-24-44	1900	31-21 N	130-04 E	045	10	Periscope	12,000	Patrol	
6-26-44	0620	31-20 N	130-02 E	145		Periscope	12,000	Trawler	
6-28-44	0253	31-52 N	127-53 E			Sight	8,000	3 Sampans	
7-1-44	0705	34-47 N	124-13 E	240		Periscope	8,000	Sampan	
7-2-44	1007	34-54 N	124-08 E			Periscope	12,000	2 motor trawler	
7-4-44	0400-0700	35-35 N	125-51 E			Sight	1,000 – 10,000	37 Sampans	
7-5-44	0312	36-45 N	125-10 E			Sight	8,000	Sampan	
7-6-44	0459	38-11 N	123-39 E			Sight		Sampan	
7-6-44	2115	36-44 N	123-51 E			Sight	8,000	Sampan	
7-7-44	2155	32-29 N	126-35 E			Sight	10,000	Killer Group	
7-8-44	2252	29-44 N	129-52 E			Sight		2 Patrols	
7-8-44	2333	29-44 N	130-05 E			Sight		3 Sampans	

Aircraft Contacts (Revised)

Contact Number		1	2	3	4	5	6	7	8
S	Date	6/26	6/27	6/27	6/27	7/7	7/7	7/9	7/10
U	Zone Time	1803	1008	1608	1758	0427	1914	0839	1031
B	Lat	31-20 N	31-00 N	31-03 N	31-03 N	34-33 N	32-50 N	29-45 N	30-05 N
M	Long	130 E	129-30 E	129-15 E	129-13 E	124-18 E	125-50 E	133-34 E	141-12 E
A	Speed	3 kts	3 kts	3 kts	3 kts	19 kts	19 kts	16 kts	18 kts
R	Course	180 T	270 T	278 T	270	180	128	090 T	090 T
I	Trim	Per.	Per.	Per.	Per.	Surf.	Surf.	Surf.	Surf.
N									
E	Time Since SD Search	None this patrol				None this patrol	None this patrol	None this patrol	None this patrol
	Number	1	1	1	1	1	1	1	1
A	Type	Betty	Betty	Lily	Float Pete	Betty	Betty	Flying boat	Trans.
I									
R	Prob Mission	Pat.	Pat.	Pat.	Pat.	Pat.	Pat.	Pat.	Pat.
C	Contacted by:	Per.	Per.	Per.	Per.	Sight	Sight	Sight	Sight
R	I.R.	2 mi.	8 mi.	8 mi.	6 mi.	12 mi.	12 mi.	14 mi.	10 mi.
A	Elev. Angle	5°	5°	2°	5°	2°	4°	6°	8°
F	Detected?	ND	ND	ND	ND	ND	ND	ND	ND
T									
C	Sea {State	4	4	4	4	3	3	2	2
O	Sea { Br.	290	300	300	300	118	343½	000	335
N	Visibility	8 mi.	15 mi.	15 mi.	15 mi.	15 mi.	15 mi.	15 mi.	30 mi.
D	Clouds {Ht	25,000	6,000	10,000	10,000	20,000	20,000	25,000	10,000
I	{% overcast	9	7	7	7	1	6	5	9
T	Moon:	Daytime	Daytime	Daytime	Daytime	Daytime	Daytime	Daytime	Daytime

Type of S/M Camouflage on this patrol Light Gray

ENCLOSURE (A)

U.S.S. *Tang* (SS 306)   Torpedo Attack No. 1   Patrol No. Three
Time: 2353 (-9)   Date: 24 June 1944   Lat: 32-30 N
                                                      Long: 129-35 E

TARGET DATA – DAMAGE INFLICTED

Ship Sunk: 1 large freighter 7,500 tons.
Damage determined by: Observed two torpedoes hit and ship sink
Target Data: Draft: 29'   Course: 000° Speed: 10 Range: 2,600.
Own Ship: Course: 292° Speed: 4   Depth: Surf.   Angle: 0
Type Attack: Night Surface.

FIRE CONTROL AND TORPEDO DATA #1

Tube No.	1	2	3
Track Angle	120° S	122° S	123° S
Gyro Angle	009	011	012
Depth Set	10'	10'	10'
Hit or Miss	Hit	Miss	Hit
Erratic	No	Yes	No
Mk. Torpedo	23	23	23
Serial No.	41607	41649	49342
Mk. Exploder	6 - 4	6 - 4	6 - 4
Serial No.	3500	177	1365
Actuation	Contact	—	—
Mk. Warhead	16 - 1	16 - 1	16 - 1
Serial No.	10511	13886	12235
Explosive	Torpex	Torpex	Torpex
Firing Interval	11 Sec.	11 Sec.	
Type Spread	Divergent point of aim.		
Sea Conditions	Flat Calm		
Overhaul Activity	Submarine Base, Pearl Harbor, T.H.		

U.S.S. *Tang* (SS 306)   Torpedo Attack No. 2   Patrol No. Three
Time: 2354 (-9)   Data: 24 June 1944   Lat: 32-30 N
                                                  Long: 129-35 E

TARGET DATA – DAMAGE INFLICTED

Description of Target: 1 large tanker, (EU) *Genyo Maru* class,
                          10,020 tons.
Ship Sunk: 1 large tanker – 10,000 tons
Damage Determined by: Observed two torpedoes hit and ship sink.
Target Data: Draft: 30'   Course: 000° Speed: 10   Range: 2,450
Own Data: Course: 292° Speed: 4   Depth: Surf. Angle: 0
Type Attack: Night Surface.

FIRE CONTROL AND TORPEDO DATA #2

Tube No.	4	5	6
Track Angle	109° S	000	002
Depth Set	10'	10'	10'
Hit or Miss	Hit	Hit	Miss
Erratic	No	No	No
Mk. Torpedo	23	23	23
Serial No.	49488	41074	49303
Mk. Exploder	6 - 4	6 - 4	6 - 4
Serial No.	11570	6941	1704
Actuation	Contact	Contact	Contact
Mk. Warhead	16 - 1	16 - 1	16 - 1
Serial No.	13884	2734	3347
Explosive	Torpex	Torpex	Torpex
Firing Interval	9 Sec.		10 Sec.
Type Spread	Divergent point of aim.		
Sea Conditions	Flat calm		
Overhaul Activity	Submarine Base, Pearl Harbor, T.H.		

U.S.S. *Tang* (SS 306)   Torpedo Attack No. 3   Patrol No. Three
Time: 0551 (-9)   Date: 27 June 1944   Lat: 31-12 N
                                                     Long: 130-12 E

TARGET DATA – DAMAGE INFLICTED

Description of Target: Medium freighter, (EU) *Ehime Maru* 4,469-4,747
Ship Sunk: None.
Target Data: Draft: 8' Course: 090° Speed: 8 Range: 1,950
Own Data: Course: 180° Speed: 3 Depth: 64' Angle: ½° rise.
Type Attack: Day submerged.

FIRE CONTROL AND TORPEDO DATA #3

Tube No.	7	8	9	10
Track Angle	106° S	107° S	108° S	109° S
Gyro Angle	195°	157°	198°	199°
Depth Set	6'	6'	6'	6'
Hit or Miss	Miss	Miss	Miss	Miss
*Erratic	No?	Yes?	No?	Yes?
Mk. Torpedo	18 - 1	18 - 1	18 - 1	18 - 1
Serial No.	54486	54453	54470	54568
Mk. Exploder	4-2	4-2	4-2	4-2
Serial No.	7956	7962	8000	8025
Actuation	—	—	—	—
Mk. Warhead	18	18	18	18
Serial No.	2243	2297	2275	2269
Explosive	Torpex	Torpex	Torpex	Torpex
Firing Interval	10 Sec.	12 Sec.	11 Sec.	
Type Spread	Divergent point of aim.			
Sea Conditions	Calm			
Overhaul Activity	Submarine Base, Pearl Harbor, T.H.			

*Two torpedoes made surface runs. Unable to determine which two.

U.S.S. *Tang* (SS 306)   Torpedo Attack No. 4A   Patrol No. Three
Time: 1759 (-8)   Date: 29 June 1944   Lat: 34-27 N
                                                   Long: 124-35 E

TARGET DATA – DAMAGE INFLICTED

Description of Target: 1 medium freighter, (EC) *Tazan Maru*, 5,464 tons
Ship Sunk: None
Target Data: Draft: 8' Course: 255° Speed: 7   Range: 1,600
Own Data: Course: 330° Speed: 3   Depth: 62' Angle: 0
Type Attack: Day Submerged.

FIRE CONTROL AND TORPEDO DATA #4A

Tube No.	1	2
Track Angle	103° P	106° P
Gyro Angle	002°	359°
Depth	10'	10'
Hit or Miss	Miss	Miss
Erratic	No	No
Mk. Torpedo	23	23
Serial No.	61671	49675
Mk. Exploder	6 - 4	6 - 4
Serial No.	8012	18511
Actuation	—	—
Mk. Warhead	16 - 1	16 - 1
Serial No.	10323	3808
Explosive	Torpex	Torpex
Firing Interval	15 Sec.	
Type Spread	Divergent point of aim.	
Sea Conditions	Rough	
Overhaul Activity	Submarine Base, Pearl Harbor, T.H.	

U.S.S. *Tang* (SS 306)   Torpedo Attack No. 4B   Patrol No. Three
Time: 0101   Date: 30 June 1944   Lat: 35-03 N
                                                           Long: 125-08 E

TARGET DATA – DAMAGE INFLICTED

Description of Target: Same as 4A.
Ship Sunk: 1 Freighter, (EC) *Tazan Maru*, 5,464 tons.
Damage Determined by: Observed torpedo hit, ship break in two and sink.
Target Data: Draft: 8' Course: 075° Speed: 9   Range: 750
Own Data: Course: 345° Speed: 0   Depth: Surf. Angle: 0
Type Attack: Night Surface.

FIRE CONTROL AND TORPEDO DATA #4B

Tube No.	5
Track Angle	092° S
Gyro Angle	354°
Depth Set	6'
Hit or Miss	Hit
Erratic	No
Mk. Torpedo	23
Serial No.	61726
Mk. Exploder:	6 - 4
Serial No.	17841
Actuation	Contact
Mk. Warhead	16 - 1
Serial No.	11025
Explosive	Torpex
Firing Interval	—
Type Spread	—
Sea Conditions	Rough
Overhaul Activity	Submarine Base, Pearl Harbor, T.H.

U.S.S. *Tang* (SS 306)   Torpedo Attack No. 5   Patrol No. Three
Time: 1444 (-8)   Date: 1 July 1944   Lat: 34-27 N
                                                      Long: 123-46 E

TARGET DATA – DAMAGE INFLICTED

Description of Target: 1 Escort freighter, (EU) *Amakasu Maru*,
                         1,852 - 1,961 tons.
Ship Sunk: 1 Escort freighter, 2,000 tons.
Damage Determined by: Heard torpedo hit, observed ship sink.
Target Data: Draft: 17½'   Course: 240°   Speed: 10   Range: 1,300
Own Data: Course: 150°   Speed: 3   Depth: 65'   Angle: ½° rise.
Type Attack: Day submerged.

FIRE CONTROL AND TORPEDO DATA #5

Tube No.	7	8
Track Angle	096° P	099° P
Gyro Angle	174°	171°
Depth Set	6'	6'
Hit or Miss	Miss	Hit
Erratic	No	No
Mk. Torpedo	18 - 1	18 - 1
Serial No.	54475	54697
Mk. Exploder	4 - 2	4 - 2
Serial No.	7936	7950
Actuation	—	Contact
Mk. Warhead	18	18
Serial No.	1962	2340
Explosive	Torpex	Torpex
Firing Interval	10 Sec.	
Type Spread	Divergent point of aim.	
Sea Conditions	Calm, slight swell.	
Overhaul Activity	Submarine Base, Pearl Harbor, T.H.	

U.S.S. *Tang* (SS 306)   Torpedo Attack No. 6   Patrol No. Three
Time: 2247 (-8)   Date: 1 July 1944   Lat: 34-33 N[6]
                                                 Long: 125-12 E

TARGET DATA – DAMAGE INFLICTED

Description of Target: 1 Medium freighter,
                         (EU) *Samarang Maru*, 3,802 - 4,070 tons.
Ship Sunk: Freighter, 4,000 tons.
Damage Determined by: Observed torpedo hit, ship explode and sink.
Target Data: Draft: 24' Course: 120   Speed: 9½   Range: 500
Own Data: Course: 210   Speed: 2   Depth: 62   Angle: 0
Type Attack: Night Submerged.

FIRE CONTROL AND TORPEDO DATA #6

Tube No.	1	3
Track Angle	90° P	102° P
Gyro Angle	000°	348°
Depth Set	6'	6'
Hit or Miss	Hit	Miss
Mk. Torpedo	23[7]	23
Serial No.	41368	41260
Mk. Exploder	6 - 4	6 - 4
Serial No.	12391	1796
Actuation	Contact	—
Mk. Warhead	16 - 1	16 - 1
Serial No.	13869	13425
Explosive	Torpex	Torpex
Firing Interval	12 Sec.	
Type Spread	Divergent point of aim.	
Sea Conditions	Flat calm	
Overhaul Activity	Submarine Base, Pearl Harbor, T.H.	

---

[6] 34-33 N: In his book *Clear the Bridge*, O'Kane gave this position as 34°-38' N.
[7] Mark 23: In the narrative, these two torpedoes are reported as being Mark 14 types and not Mark 23. The only actual difference between the two types was that the Mark 14 had both high and low speed settings, while the Mark 23 was a single (high) speed model. The low speed setting on the Mark 14 was rarely used in any case.

U.S.S. *Tang* (SS 306)   Torpedo Attack No. 7   Patrol No. Three
Time: 0626 (-8)   Data: 4 July 1944   Lat: 35-22 N
   Long: 125-56 E

TARGET DATA – DAMAGE INFLICTED

Description of Target: (EU) *Kurosio Maru* class (XAV).
Ship Sunk: (EU) *Kurosio Maru* Class (XAV),
   10,000 tons gross,
   16,000 Standard displacement.
Damage Determined by: Heard two torpedoes hit, observed ship sink in
   two sections.
Target Data: Draft: 29½' Course: 175° Speed: 3   Range: 2,500
Own Data: Course: 100   Special: 3 Depth: 64' Angle: 0
Type Attack: Day Submerged.

FIRE CONTROL AND TORPEDO DATA #7

Tube No.	1	3	5
Track Angle	105° S	107° S	109° S
Gyro Angle	002	004	006
Depth Set	8'	8'	8'
Hit or Miss	Hit	Hit	Miss
Erratic	No	No	No
Mk. Torpedo	23	23	23
Serial No.	41526	41446	41041
Mk. Exploder	6 - 4	6 - 4	6 - 4
Serial No.	11488	12728	2679
Actuation	Contact	Contact	—
Mk. Warhead	16 - 1	16 - 1	16 - 1
Serial No.	13895	11994	2324
Explosive	Torpex	Torpex	Torpex
Firing Interval	8 Sec.	11 Sec.	
Type Spread	Divergent point of aim.		
Sea Conditions	Flat calm.		
Overhaul Activity	Submarine Base, Pearl Harbor, T.H.		

U.S.S. *Tang* (SS 306)   Torpedo Attack No. 8   Patrol No. Three
Time: 2128 (-8)   Date: 4 July 1944   Lat: 36-05 N
                                                   Long: 125-48 E

TARGET DATA – DAMAGE INFLICTED

Description of Target: 1 modern large ore ship,
                          (EC) *Ama-auka Maru* (not listed)
Ship Sunk: 1 large ore ship, (EC) *Ama-auka Maru*, 7,000 - 10,000 tons,
      pending questioning of prisoner by an interpreter.
Damage Determined by: Observed one torpedo hit, and ship sink by
                         the middle.
Target Data: Draft: 20' Course: 045° Speed: 9½   Range: 910
Own Data: Course: 330° Speed: 3   Depth: 65' Angle: 0
Type Attack: Night Submerged.

FIRE CONTROL AND TORPEDO DATA #8

Tube No.	5	6
Track Angle	98° S	107° S
Gyro Angle	357°	003°
Depth Set	8'	8'
Hit or Miss	Hit	Miss
Erratic	No	No
Mk. Torpedo	23	23
Serial No.	46135	49703
Mk. Exploder	6 - 4	6 - 4
Serial No.	2384	7107
Actuation	Contact	—
Mk. Warhead	11303	11398
Explosive	Torpex	Torpex
Firing Interval	9 Sec.	
Type Spread	Divergent point of aim.	
Sea Conditions	Calm	
Overhaul Activity:	Submarine Base, Pearl Harbor, T.H.	

U.S.S. *Tang* (SS 306)   Torpedo Attack No. 9   Patrol No. Three
Time: 0320 (-8)   Date: 6 July 1944   Lat: 33-40 N
                                                       Long: 123-40 E

TARGET DATA – DAMAGE INFLICTED

Description of Target: 1 medium freighter, (EU) *Osaka Maru*,
                      3,741 - 4,106
Ship Sunk: 1 Medium freighter, (EU) *Osaka Maru*, 4,000 tons.
Target Data: Draft: 24'   Course: 317° Speed: 9   Range: 900
Own Data: Course: 040   Speed: 3   Depth: 64'   Angle: ½° rise
Type Attack: Night Submerged.

FIRE CONTROL AND TORPEDO DATA #9

Tube No.	9	10
Track Angle	86° S	91° S
Gyro Angle	185°	190°
Depth Set	6'	6'
Hit or Miss	Hit	Hit
Erratic	No	No
Mk. Torpedo	18 - 1	18 - 1
Serial No.	54470	54617
Mk. Exploder	4 - 2	4 -2
Serial No.	7997	8016
Actuation	Contact	Contact
Mk. Warhead	18	18
Serial No.	1588	2304
Explosive	Torpex	Torpex
Firing Interval	8 Sec.	
Type Spread	Divergent point of aim	
Sea Conditions	Flat calm	
Overhaul Activity:	Submarine Base, Pearl Harbor, T.H.	

FS5-82/A16-3   Submarine Division Sixty-Two

Serial 024   Care of Fleet Post Office,
                                              San Francisco, California,
C-O-N-F-I-D-E-N-T-I-A-L   17 July 1944.

First Endorsement to
U.S.S. *Tang* – Report
of War Patrol No. 3
dated 14 July 1944.

From: The Commander Submarine Division Sixty-Two.
To: The Commander in Chief, U.S. Fleet.
Via: (1) The Commander Submarine Force, Pacific Fleet,
                 Subordinate Command, Navy Number 1504.
             (2) The Commander Submarine Force, Pacific Fleet.
             (3) The Commander in Chief, U.S. Pacific Fleet.

Subject: U.S.S. *Tang* (SS306) – Report of Third War Patrol.

1.   The *Tang* on this, her third war patrol, sixteen days after entering her assigned area, the East China and Yellow Seas, had fired 24 torpedoes in ten attacks and sunk 6 ships for a total of 39,000 estimated tons with 12 hits. The entire patrol covered a period of 36 days.

2.   (a) Attack No. 1 and 2. On the night of 24 June, *Tang* on the surface tore into a convoy of six large ships with at least 16 escorts and with six torpedoes (three at each) sank a 7,500 ton freighter and a 10,000 ton tanker[8]. Mark 23 torpedoes were fired at an average range of 2,500 yards, on 120 and 110 degree starboard tracks with 10 foot depth setting. One torpedo was observed to run erratically.

(b) Attack No. 3. Soon after dawn on 26 June an SJ contact at 8,000 yards provided a target in the form of a medium sized unescorted freighter. *Tang* made a quick end around run, submerged and fired four Mark 18's from stern tubes with a depth setting of six feet on a 100 degree starboard track, range 1,950. Two of the torpedoes broached and made surface runs alerting the target in time to allow torpedoes to be avoided. The freighter ran for cover while *Tang* surfaced and cleared area just ahead of a late arriving patrol boat.

---

[8] Postwar, the Japanese revealed that this six-torpedo salvo actually sank two additional freighters, making the total for this patrol ten ships instead of the eight originally credited.

(c) <u>Attack 4A and 4B</u>. Just prior to noon on 29 June, while patrolling submerged an unescorted medium freighter estimated at 3,500 tons was sighted on a course which prevented *Tang* reaching a firing position. *Tang* turned away, surfaced, made end around and four hours later submerged and fired two Mark 23's on a 90 port track, range 1,250 yards with depth set at 10 feet. Both missed (probably passed under ship). Three close depth charges followed, one of which detonated under circumstances which might point to use of a time delay feature for shallow water. *Tang* surfaced and chased for an hour before regaining contact on SJ. Made an end around and at a 750 yard range on the surface, fired one Mark 14 "feeler" set at six feet on a 92 degree track. This torpedo broke the ship in two and it sank under the eyes of *Tang*'s crew. The apparent efficiency of *Tang*'s camouflage job is noted with interest.

(d) <u>Attack No. 5</u>. On the morning of 1 July 1944 *Tang* on surface sighted and attacked a 4,000 ton medium freighter and a 2,000 ton escort freighter. Submerging for periscope attack she fired two Mark 18's at the escort-freighter range 1,250, 100 port track with depth set at six feet. One hit and the ship was observed to sink in a minute and 20 seconds. The freighter reversed course and *Tang* trailed successfully until dusk when she surfaced, made end around, submerged again and in

(e) <u>Attack No. 6</u>. Sank the freighter with one hit out of two Mark 23's fired at a 500 yard range on a 90 port track with depth set at six feet. The manner in which this ship blew up indicates a cargo of munitions.

(f) <u>Attack No. 7</u>. At dawn on 4 July 1944 *Tang* made an end around on the masts of a ship and dove one hour later to continue the approach on what developed into a 15,000 ton (XAV) seaplane tender or aircraft transport. With rapidly shoaling water and the keel about to scrape the bottom *Tang* backed down and fired three Mark 23's, range 2,600, 90 starboard track with depth set at 8 feet. Two hits sank this ship and *Tang* surfaced to clear the area in the midst of 34 fishing boat with close to 50 survivors thrashing about in the water and in large life boats.

(g) <u>Attack No. 8</u>. In the late afternoon of the same day, 4 July, smoke was sighted and closed until picked up by radar at 18,500 yard and sighted at 15,000. After tracking to determine his zig plan a submerged radar periscope approach resulted in the firing of *Tang*'s last two Mark 23's at a 900 yard range, 90 starboard track with depth set at 8 feet. One hit struck this ship and *Tang* surfaced and took aboard the one visible survivor and a life raft. The sunken ship from observation and questioning of the prisoner was estimated to be an ore ship converted from a modern tanker hull of about 10,000 tons.

(h) <u>Attack No. 9</u>. On the night of 5 July under a full moon an SJ radar contact at 29,000 yards was tracked out to 32,000 yards and then an end around run made which placed the *Tang* seven miles ahead of the target. In a submerged radar periscope attack the last two torpedoes, Mark 18's from the stern tubes, were fired at 900 yards range with a 90 starboard track, depth setting 6 feet. Both torpedoes hit and two minutes later on surfacing only floating wreckage and broken life boats remained from a medium freighter of 4,000 tons.

3. This, the third consecutive outstanding patrol turned in by the *Tang*, was characterized by the same aggressive determined and efficient fighting spirit that was so noticeable in her first and second patrols. To her enviable record of sinking 5 ships totaling 41,969 tons on her first patrol and the efficient rescuing of 22 naval aviators on her second patrol the *Tang* now adds 8 more ships sunk for an additional 59,000 tons on this patrol.

4. Twelve hits out of 24 torpedoes fired, three of which were seen to run erratic, is an excellent score in any league and one which the *Tang*'s Control Party may well be proud of.

5. Material condition on return from patrol was excellent. Refit will be accomplished by Division 62 Relief Crew assisted by the Submarine Base Midway.

6. The Commanding Officer, Officers and crew are most heartily congratulated on this very outstanding patrol. It is recommended that *Tang* be credited with inflicting the following damage up the enemy:

SUNK

1 Freighter (*Aobasan Maru* class) (EU) (Attack #1)	7,500 tons
1 Tanker (*Genyo Maru* class) (EU) (Attack #2)	10,000 tons
1 Freighter (*Tazan Maru* class) (EC) (Attack #4B)	5,500 tons
1 Escort-Freighter (*Amakasu Maru* class) (Attack #5)	2,000 tons
1 Freighter (*Samarang Maru* class) (EU) (Attack #6)	4,000 tons
1 (XAV) (*Kurosio Maru* class) (EU) (Attack #7)	16,000 tons
1 Tanker Hull, Ore ship (*Ama-auka Maru*) (EC) (Attack #8)	10,000 tons
1 Freighter (*Osaka maru* class) (EU) (Attack #9) TOTAL	4,000 tons 59,000 tons

J.W. WILL.

A16-3   Commander Submarine Force, Pacific Fleet
               Sub Ordinate Command, Navy No. 1504.   Mc
Serial: 0120

C-O-N-F-I-D-E-N-T-I-A-L   Care of Fleet Post Office,
                                 San Francisco, California,
                                 19 July 1944.

<u>Second Endorsement</u> to
U.S.S. *Tang* – Report of War
Patrol No. 3 dated 14
July 1944

From: The Commander Submarine Force, Pacific Fleet,
               Subordinate Command, Navy Number 1504.
To: The Commander-in-Chief, United States Fleet.
Via: (1) The Commander Submarine Force, Pacific Fleet.
             (2) The Commander-in-Chief, U.S. Pacific Fleet.

Subject: U.S.S. *Tang* (SS306) – Report of Third War Patrol.

1.   Forwarded, concurring in all remarks contained in the first endorsement. This outstanding ship has, in two offensive patrols, sunk a record total of over 100,000 tons of enemy shipping and rescued 22 naval aviators on her other patrol since joining the fleet.

2.   The use of echo ranging just prior to firing is noted and undoubtedly paid dividends. No indications of alerting the enemy developed. The use of additional lookouts rather the SD radar for plane detection and only periodic use of the SJ no doubt accounts for the additional freedom of motion through lack of detection of *Tang* by enemy planes and surface vessels previously reported as homing on this equipment. Information gained by use of the APR-1 radar detector was extremely valuable and the early installation of this equipment in all fleet submarines is urged.

The heartiest of congratulations are extended the Commanding Officer, Officers and men of the U.S.S. *Tang* upon the completion of this, another outstanding patrol.

                              C.D. Edmonds
Copy to:
     CSD 62
     CO *Tang*

Submarine Force, Pacific Fleet   heh

FF12-10/A16-3(15)(1)

         Care of Fleet Post Office,

Serial [0510]   San Francisco, California,

         24 July 1944.

CONFIDENTIAL

Third Endorsement to   Note: This report will be
Tang Report of   destroyed prior to
Third War Patrol.   entering patrol area.

ComSubPac Patrol Report No. <u>478</u>.
U.S.S. *Tang* - Third War Patrol.

From: The Commander Submarine Force, Pacific Fleet.
To: The Commander-in-Chief, United States Fleet.
Via: The Commander-in-Chief, U.S. Pacific Fleet.

Subject: U.S.S. *Tang* (SS306) – Report of Third War Patrol.
             (8 June to 14 July 1944).

1.   The third war patrol of the *Tang* was conducted in the East China Sea and Yellow Sea Areas.

2.   This patrol was an outstanding example of excellent judgment, expert area analysis, bull-dog tenacity, and severe damage to the enemy. In a period of 12 days the *Tang* made nine torpedo attacks, sinking eight vessels. Each attack was carefully planned and brilliantly executed. This patrol sets a record for submarines operating in the Central Pacific Area as to the amount of damage inflicted upon the enemy.

3.   The *Tang* was one of three submarines assigned to work in the area West and North of the Japanese Empire. This was not a coordinated attack group, but a group designated to work adjacent areas, close together, and planned in order to pass contacts from one to the other.

4.   It is of note that many radar contacts were made using the APR-1 detector.

5.   This patrol is designated as "Successful" for Combat Insignia award.

6.   The Commander Submarine Force, Pacific Fleet, congratulates the Commanding Officer, officers, and crew for this very outstanding war patrol. The *Tang* is further congratulated for the outstanding performance of its three

war patrols during which the *Tang* has sunk 13 enemy vessels for 97,969 tons on two of them and rescued 22 aviators on the other. The *Tang* is credited with having inflicted the following damage upon the enemy:

SUNK

1 – Large Freighter (*Aobasan Maru* class) (EU)	– 7,500 tons	(Attack No. 1)
1 – Large Tanker (*Genyo Maru* class) (EU)	– 10,000 tons	(Attack No. 2)
1 – Freighter (*Tazan Maru* class) (EC)	– 5,500 tons	(Attack No. 4A)
1 – Small Freighter (*Amakasu Maru* class) (EU)	– 2,000 tons	(Attack No. 5)
1 – Medium Freighter (*Samarang Maru* class) (EC)	– 4,000 tons	(Attack No. 6)
1 – Seaplane Tender (*Kurosio*) (EU)	– 16,000 tons	(Attack No. 7)
1 – Ore Ship (*Yamaoka Maru*) (EC)*	– 7,000 tons	(Attack No. 8)
1 – Medium Freighter (*Osaka Maru* class) (EU)	– 4,000 tons	(Attack No. 9)
TOTAL	56,000 tons	

*The name and the tonnage of this ship was obtained from the prisoner picked up by the *Tang*.

Distribution:
(Complete Reports)

Cominch	(7)	C.A. Lockwood, Jr.
CNO	(5)	
CinCpac	(6)	
Intel.Cen.Pac.Ocean Areas	(1)	
ComServPac	(1)	
ComSubLant	(6)	
S/M School, NL	(2)	
ComSoPac	(2)	
ComSoWesPac	(1)	
ComSubSoWesPac	(2)	
CTF 72	(2)	
ComForPac	(1)	
ComSubsPac	(40)	
SUBAD, MI	(2)	
ComSubsPacSubOrdCom	(3)	

All Squadron and Div.
   Commanders, SubsPac   (2)
ComSubsTrainPac   (2)
All Submarines, SubsPac   (1)

E.L. Hymes, 2nd,
Flag Secretary

Patrol Four, 31 July 1944 – 3 September 1944

U.S.S. *Tang* (SS 306)
c/o Fleet Post Office,
San Francisco, Calif.

A16-3
Serial 013
CONFIDENTIAL   3 September, 1944

From: The Commanding Officer.
To: The Commander-in-Chief, United States Fleet.
Via: The Commander Submarine Division 141.
             The Commander Submarine Squadron 14.
             The Commander Submarine Force, Pacific Fleet.
             The Commander-in-Chief, U.S. Pacific Fleet.

Subject: U.S.S. *Tang* (SS 306), Report of Fourth War Patrol.

Enclosures: (A) Subject Report.
             (B) Track Chart (Comsubpac only).

1.   Enclosure (A), covering the fourth war patrol of this vessel conducted in Japanese Empire waters during the period 31 July, 1944 to 3 September, 1944, is forwarded herewith.

R.H. O'Kane

(A) PROLOGUE

Returned from third war patrol July fourteenth. The refit by SubDiv 62 and Submarine Base, Midway, completed on the twenty-fourth, is considered our finest to date. Conducted normal training and departed July thirty-first.

(B) NARRATIVE

July 31 (+12) – August 7 (-9)

1555 Underway for areas four and five at two engine speed. Conducted usual training dives and fire control drills, and enjoyed yachting weather.

August 8 (-9)

0950 Dived a half hour to avoid a bomber sighted at about eight miles.

1410 Dived an hour for another bomber about ten miles away.

2351 Sighted Mikura Shima in the Nampo Shoto, but because of known radar installations nearby, proceeded to Inamba Shima[1], a small pinnacle, for checking our SJ.

August 9 (-9)

Conducted submerged patrol near Inamba Shima in the vicinity of numerous plotted contacts. Continuous searching, with

1900 periodic sweeps at forty feet finally located what might have been smoke beyond Zeni Su, so on surfacing proceeded to the northwest to investigate. No contact was made, but as all the surrounding areas were vacant, closed the coast in the bight west of Omae Saki for submerged patrol at dawn.

August 10 (-9)

0441 Dived six miles from the beach and continued closing the coast. A few minutes later sighted single mast and superstructure of an apparent patrol boat which continued its sweep down the coast.

0903 Sighted a large engine-aft ship against the beach, escorted by three bombers. We were already on his beam six thousand yards away, so except for closing the traffic route, our approach served only to impress our OOD's with the necessity of sticking one's eyeballs on the beach to pick out the shipping.
Attack No. 1

1010 Within an hour of having secured from battle stations for this first ship, and having avoided another patrol by continuing in, sighted an old type

---

[1] Inamba Shima: O'Kane called this island Inamba Jima in *Clear The Bridge!* These are alternate names for the same small island, located at 33°-30' N, 139°-18' E.

loaded tanker right against the beach headed for Omae Saki. As four bombers were the only escorts, took a sounding to find we were still in forty fathoms. A standard speed approach closed him to 1,200 yards where with

1034 echo and stadimeter ranges checking, fired three Mk. 23 torpedoes spread his length by constant bearings, 100 starboard track, speed 8.5, set at eight feet, gyros near zero. No hits. No explosions on the beach three thousand yard away. Two minutes after firing the tanker, alerted, reversed course away, so commenced evasion, thoroughly expecting bombs or several depth charges. We rolled on the bottom a little at eighty feet during our turn to evade, but reached deep water and commenced periscope patrol in [deeper water].

1500 Very distant counter attack commences.

1920 Surfaced north of Daio Saki, and staying clear of its 252 MC radar, proceeded down the 100 fathom curve past Miki Saki searching for any night shipping.

August 11 (-9)

0418 Having doubled back to Miki Saki, dived three miles west of the point, then closed to intercept any morning shipping.

0515 When visibility was just becoming good enough through the periscope, sighted smoke against the beach and the bow wake of an escort. Before we could reach an approach course, the escort and a large engine-aft freighter ducked around Miki Saki and into Kada Wan, thence down the coast.

Patrol activity increased steadily with one pinger generally in sight, an in-shore patrol proceeding back and forth a thousand yards off Miki Saki, and a motor boat resembling a landing barge with six lookouts making a nuisance of itself.

1244 After ducking for a modern looking gunboat loaded with depth charges, heard extremely loud pinging coming up the coast. The A/S vessel was not as big as his ping, but by coming straight to Mike Saki, then changing course to southward, he forced us off the fifty fathom curve as we kept our stern to him. His method became apparent when a tanker came out of

1355 Kada An and ducked around Miki Saki with the *Tang* hopelessly out of position for attack.

1500 With changing tide, fogging periscopes nearly ruined the rest of our day for we were spotted by the motor boat when longer exposures became necessary. He was extremely difficult to shake, but on sighting smoke, a half hour run at standard speed into Owashi Wan left him out on the 80 fathom curve. This put us in about forty fathoms of water, on the route followed by the tanker, and on their most probably track.

Attacks No. 2 and 3

The smoke, which had been in two columns, developed into two mast-funnel-mast split superstructure freighters in column. They were escorted well to seaward by the gunboat previously sighted, and by a smaller escort on the other bow. During the remainder of the approach, the leading ship was identified (EC) as of the *Biyo Maru* class, page 220, ONI 208-J (rev'd), and the second, about two thirds her size, as similar (EU) to the *Akasi Maru*, page 230. Both ships were heavily loaded.

1740 When in position 1,700 yards on the enemy's beam, just prior to giving a final set-up, sound reported fast screws on our port quarter. A quick look showed our gunboat coming in fast about a thousand yards away, evidently warned by the motor boat of our presence.

1741 Fired three Mk. 23 torpedoes at the leading freighter, range 1,800, 110 starboard track, depth setting 6 feet, spread 150' of the target's length by constant bearing, followed by a similar spread at the second freighter on an 80 starboard track. Took a quick low power sweep to observe the gunboat filling the field boiling past our stern, evidently having misjudged our course and giving the wrong lead. Reassured, swung quickly to the leading target in time to see the first torpedo hit right in the middle, evidently in his Scotch boilers[2], for he disintegrated with the explosion.

1743 On our way deep, timed our fourth and fifth torpedoes to hit the second freighter, followed by a tooth-shaking depth charge attack. As the gunboat's screws on our port bow showed his intent to turn us toward shallow water, made a full speed dash, assured by single ping soundings taken with each barrage.

Even at this speed, the twisting, scrunching, breaking-up noises were loud in the direction of the targets. After twenty-two close ones, the charges drew aft and we were

1821 able to return to periscope depth in thirty-eight minutes. The gunboat was now about 4,000 yards on our quarter, the other escort at the scene of the attacks apparently picking up survivors, and one plane was circling the area. Nothing else was in sight.

2005 Continued to seaward at five knots and surfaced at dark with depth charging still progressing and the area astern of us being swept by searchlight.

2010 Headed for Inamba Shima at 18 knots.

---

[2] Scotch Boiler: A cylindrical, horizontal fire-tube type boiler with multiple fire boxes under the water cylinder. The hot combustion gases are directed under the water cylinder, then up a "fire back" at the rear, after which they pass through horizontal fire tubes the length of the water cylinder, and are exhausted at the front of the boiler. A common steamship type due to its efficiency and relative compactness.

August 12 (-9)

0420 Commenced submerged patrol between Inamba Shima and Mikura Shima back on our schedule.

0736 Maneuvered to avoid a patrol boat and proceeded south of Mikura Shima as the Kuroshio[4] was setting us on the island.

1505 Again the enemy had succeeded in chasing us from a likely spot, for after twenty-four depth charges and continous planes and patrols, sighted distant smoke in the direction of our dawn position.

1918 As our attempts to maintain, and then to regain contact with the smoke had been futile, and even a six knot enemy ship would reach Tokyo Bay ahead of us, proceeded to the Nojima Saki – Inubo Saki area to intercept coastal traffic.

2300 Moved into Katsuura Wan three miles from the beach to insure radar contact on any shipping.

August 13 (-9)

0312 As no contact was made and the visibility dropped to zero from wood smoke rolling from the beach, withdrew for submerged patrol at dawn.

0654 Sighted distant smoke to the southeast headed for Nojima Saki and Tokyo. Four bombers and a patrol boat prevented a surface dash to get on his track, and our twelve mile approach fell short by six thousand yards of attaining a firing position.

1921 After surfacing, took one more turn up the 100 fathom curve to Inubo Saki before proceeding south to the Tori Shima area of the southern islands.

August 14 (-9)

0429 When 40 miles east of Hachijo Shima, dived to avoid detection by a patrol yacht. His maneuvering during the day prevented our usual surfacing for high periscope searches, so kept him in sight for a 4" target if better shipping did not show up. Numerous planes indicated that he may have reported us too.

1430 Surfaced to regain contact but dived in twenty minutes on the approach of a plane.

Gun Attack No. 1

1753 Surfaced to maintain contact and check all guns, then closed

1832 to seven thousand yards and commenced firing.

The enemy was tenacious and wiry, twisting and turning and closing the range at every opportunity, and though he replied only with apparent 20 MM

---

[3] Kuroshio: The Japanese current.

machine guns, he was on in deflection and not far short with a range of 4,500 yard, forcing us to haul off frequently.

It was impossible with his movements and the 4" rate of fire to stay on for more than one or two hits, and only eight sure hits were observed. These were beauts, however, demolishing his deck house aft and exploding in his side and upper works.

1926 With eighty-eight rounds expended and the enemy still under control, perhaps from control station, proceeded to the south for patrol on the following day.

August 14 (-9)
Conducted submerged periscope patrol east of Tori Shima, surfacing periodically for high periscope searches.

1339 Dived on sighting a Mavis, which dropped one depth charge thirty minutes later.

1532 Continued surface patrol.

August 17 (-9)
Patrolled as on previous day.

0736 Dived for an hour to avoid detection by a distant bomber.

1326 Dived again for a bomber.

August 18 (-9)
Patrolled as on previous day.

1310 Dived an hour for a distant aircraft, then proceeded west at three engine speed to reach Kantori Saki by the following night.

August 19 (-9)
En route Kantori Saki for close in patrol.

1304 Submerged thirty miles from the coast and continued to close submerged.

1904 On surfacing closed the coast just north of Kantori Saki to intercept any night shipping. The numerous sampans and row of lights previously reported are still in evidence, but nothing interfered with our closing to 5,000 yards from the beach, where contact with any shipping would be assured.

2347 Tracked a patrol boat as he came down the coast to seaward of us and then reversed course back toward Miki Saki.

August 20 (-9)

Continued close in radar search for shipping. 156 and 256 megacycle radar was in evidence, but it didn't seem to bite.

0450 Dived on the fifty fathom curve two miles from the beach where attack on any coastal traffic was assured.

0805 Avoided a patrol boat coming down the coast.

Attack No. 4

0947 Sighted tops and smoke of a freighter coming out of the mist from the north. As the enemy was inside the ten fathom curve, we still had to close the coast a little and dodge numerous sampans, but his escorts, two SC's, were well clear on his beam and port bow to seaward. The freighter was a modern, medium sized, engine-aft ship. With range 900, 123 port track, speed 8, gyros around 30, fired two Mk 23 torpedoes at his stack and foremast by constant bearings, depth setting six feet.

The first torpedo evidently missed astern and exploded on the beach, while the second torpedo left the tube with a clonk but did not run.

We had to take our first eight depth charges at periscope depth, but had gained deep water for the next twenty-two.

2142 Surfaced and headed around Shioko Misaki to attack the coastal traffic between this point and Ichiye Saki. Radar on 82, 99, and 216 megacycles was in evidence but nothing came of it.

August 21 (-9)

0456 Dived in deep water off Okinokura Shima and closed the beach slowly for an afternoon attack.

0855 A large ship and two escorts proceeding eastward and rounding Shiono Misaki out of reach changed our plan, and we closed the next freighter two hours later. She was a medium sized new engine-aft job with escorts well ahead, but with a 3,000 yard torpedo run, broke off the attack, as a better shot was practically assured.

Attack No. 5

After closing the beach to a twenty fathom spot off Okinokura Shima, headed west to buck a two knot easterly set.

1243 Sighted smoke, then a medium mast-funnel-mast freighter coming up the coast unbelievably close to the beach. Our approach consisted mainly of ducking the two sub chasers and whale killer escorts, and turning left for a stern shot.

1317 At a range of 1,650 yards, fired three Mark 18-1 torpedoes spread 150' of the freighter's length by constant bearings, 110 port track, depth setting six feet, gyros around 20 left. All torpedoes exploded on the beach.

We were at 200 feet, two fathoms off the bottom, when the first depth charge let go, and reached deep water twenty charges later. Our evasion at 100 turns kept everything aft including late arriving pingers.

Checks on the firing bearing with our Mark 8[4], and plot of the firing, showed everything in order. This left only the possibility of deep running torpedoes to explain our persistent misses, so decided to keep slugging and continue checking torpedoes.

On our first trip to Miki Saki we were caught napping by a freighter and escort which rounded the point just after dawn. Radar searches had shown no night traffic, so felt sure shipping might wait at Owase or Owase Wan just north of Miki

1916 and Nuki Saki. On surfacing, proceeded clear of Kantori Saki, to probe the above bay.

August 22 (-9)
Attack No. 6

0020 After passing Miki Saki, slowed, crossed the 100 fathom curve and proceeded around Kuki Saki into Owase Wan. Side lobes were confusing, but we soon found "a pip where no pip ought to be." The night was black and only the long shape of the enemy could be seen until we circled him to get him away from the land background. There he was quite visible, indentified as the gunboat who had harassed us during our first visit, topping it off with those tooth-shakers. He tracked at zero speed and was obviously anchored in about 20 fathoms two miles northwest of Miki Saki. Holding our breath, we moved in slowly to twelve hundred yards, twisted, then

0142 steadied for a straight stern shot and fired one Mark 18-1 torpedo at his middle set on three feet.

The phosphorescent wake petered out after a hundred yard run with the torpedo evidently heading down, and hit bottom with a loud rumble, timed half way to the enemy, where there should have been 250 feet of water. It was tracked by sound to this moment, but after the rumble cleared away, nothing more was heard.

0144 Fired a second Mark 18-1 torpedo set on three feet, feeling sure the enemy had been alerted by the first. It's [*sic*] wake was dimly visible directly to the target, tracked also by sound, but it passed underneath, apparently running on the deep side too.

---

[4] Mark 8: The Mark 8 Angle Solver was a circular slide rule used for manually calculating torpedo firing angles. It was used as a backup for the electro-mechanical Torpedo Data Computer (TDC) and, as in this case, to double-check the TDC results when analyzing an attack.

With one salvo of three left aft, circled for a bow shot,

0156 and with range 900, fired a Mark 23 torpedo from number 5 tube at his middle, set on zero feet. Though we were stopped and absolutely steady and the gyro angle zero, it took a thirty yard jog to the left before settling toward the target and missed astern.

Still whispering, though the last two torpedoes must

0200 have roared past him, fired a second Mark 23 torpedo from number 6 tube set on zero aimed at his gun forward. It took a jog to the left also, but settled down right for his middle.

The explosion forty seconds later was the most spectacular we've ever seen, topped by a pillar of fire and more explosions about five hundred feet in the air. There was absolutely nothing left of the gunboat.

This vessel was observed at close hand previously during daylight. She was new in appearance, flush deck, with raised gun platforms forward and amidships mounting estimated 3" double purpose guns. Aft of the midship platform was a goal post structure, possibly for use in sweeping, topped by a lookout or director platform. Her stern had very long almost horizontal depth charge racks holding fourteen counted depth charges a side, and what appeared to be Y-guns on the centerline. On observation before firing she measured between 225' and 250' in length and is estimated to have a standard displacement of 1,500 tons.

Feeling that our difficulties had been mainly in sluggish steering and depth engines, withdrew at full power to spend the day checking afterbodies of our remaining torpedoes.

After giving the steering engines a good workout to insure they were free, checked our rudder throws. On three of the six torpedoes they were three quarters to one degree heavy. With a careful trim and no pressure in the boat, swung all torpedoes and calibrated depth springs.

1900 Now confident that our last two salvos would count, headed for Omae Saki and the scene of our first attack of the patrol.

August 23 (-9)

0100 In position on the fifty fathom curve west of Omae Saki, moved slowly to the bight off Fukuda. We were six thousand yards from the beach and it is certain that no shipping passed, though navigational lights were burning.

0417 Submerged, this time in our desired position, and commenced a cautious periscope patrol. Plane activity started right after daylight followed by the first patrol a half hour later.

0803 Sighted smoke of two freighters as they rounded Omae Saki and commenced closing their track. As expected, they were practically aground, so closed to 1,000 yards from a wreck off Fukuda, undoubtedly one of our subs' handy-work. Though the escorts were clear, an unexpected zig and third previously unobserved small freighter put us underfoot. A full speed dash succeeded only in getting us clear as they boiled by our bow and stern about two hundred yards off.

0923 We had been secured from battle stations less than a half hour when an old type destroyer, four bombers, and a float plane commenced searching down the coast. At first it appeared that we'd been spotted, but his circling tactics resemble the routine sweep we'd observed off Miki Saki. Though we had our torpedoes set at two feet and he came very close, we could secure nothing but sharp tracks or large angle shots. Why his ear-splitting pinger didn't pick us up will remain a pleasant mystery.

Attack No. 7

1017 With the destroyer just clear the reason for the activity became apparent with the sighting of masts and high superstructure of a ship coming down the coast toward Omae Saki. He was escorted by a large PC or DE ahead, an SC on his bow, our aircraft previously sighted overhead, and an LST and a PC astern.

We had been forced out a little by the destroyer, and a high speed approach was necessary to insure a short firing range. It was therefore not until the angle on the bow opened ten minutes before firing that the full import of our enemy became apparent. The decks of his long superstructure were lined with men in white uniforms, as was his upper bridge.

1110 Made another five minute dash to close the track, slowed and

1118 took two echo ranges, and fired three Mark 23 torpedoes spread his length by constant bearings, 105 starboard track, range 800 yards, speed 8, depth setting six feet, then commenced swinging for a stern shot at the LST.

The first and third torpedoes hit beautifully in this short well deck forward, and the after part of this long superstructure, giving him a twenty degree down angle which he maintained as he went under with naval ensign flying.

There is no ship resembling this in any of the ONI publications, though if the *Buenos Aires Maru* on page 45 were given a raked bow and her stack cut down level with her superstructure, she would be a close approximation. She was *not*, however, a hospital ship[5]. The gross tonnage of this vessel would be in the neighborhood of 10,000 tons and her standard displacement 15,000.

1121 Our LST headed for the beach and someone dropped two depth charges, not close, which permitted us to get two soundings and clear out at

[5] *Bueno Aires Maru* herself had been designated as a hospital ship, and as such would have been immune from attack. O'Kane included this statement to emphasize that, while of similar design, this was a different ship and a legitimate military target.

100 turns. For once, depth charging the submarine seemed to take second priority, undoubtedly as survivors were picked up, for it was ten minutes before they started to rain. We had then reached deep water, and two hours at high speed, then gradual slowing, kept everything astern, including a multi-ship echo ranging search during the remainder of the day.

1907 Following our hit and run policy, commenced a full power dash to round Shiono Misaki for another crack at the coastal traffic before a waxing moon made evasion difficult.

August 24 (-9)

Radar on 82, 96, and 256 megacycles was again in evidence near Shiono Misaki, but it appears to be poor, or in port early warning installations.

0336 Sighted a ship on the SJ at 10,000 yards about on the 100 fathom curve. After tracking it at six knots and gaining position there, picked up and sighted another ship close to the beach. As this latter seemed to be the larger and the

0428 former probably an escort, switched approach and dived for a periscope attack in the dawn that was breaking. When the generated range was 3,000 he commenced signaling with yardarm blinkers, then turned away displaying a super load of depth charges and efficient looking guns. Though we had our tubes ready for this patrol, he wandered shoreward, never giving us a setup. It appeared that he had been relieved by a second patrol which occupied our attention for the next two hours,

0950 and too late we saw him lead a modern medium sized diesel tanker out of Kazampo, just east of Ichiye Saki, and head for Shiono Misaki hugging the coast.

Activity increased toward noon with the passage down the coast of a *Hishun Maru* class patrol with two stripes on his stack. Within an hour sighted smoke beyond Ataki Saki, and assuming our escort commander would soon be back with the freighter, moved in to the forty fathom curve. He was there all right on the next observation with two large freighters astern. They were both riding high and practically on the beach, escorted astern by a similar patrol, on their beam by two worming destroyers, and five PC's fanned out to the 100 fathom curve. Their echo ranging frequencies varied from about 500 cycles, nicely audible on the JP and sounding like a pile driver on the lowest limit of the JK, to above the upper limit of the JK at 37 KCs.

Convinced that this was a little too much for a twenty fathom shot with our last three torpedoes, slithered under the inboard PC, a fathom or two off the bottom, and reached deep water with only one token depth charge.

1930 As our presence was at least suspected in this location, commenced a high speed run around Shiono and Kantori Saki to attack off Nigishima Saki after daylight. This point lies about five miles southwest of Miki Saki and is tipped by a small island three hundred yards off the beach around which shipping must pass.

Our previous observations showed that the motorboat patrols did not range this far from Miki Saki. If the echo ranging patrols could be avoided below the gradients in the fifty fathoms available without moving off their track, position for attack could be assured.

2342 Closing Nigishima was not without incident however, for with lookout and radar efficiency poor in frequent rain squalls, suddenly sighted a submarine on our beam parallel to us, unbelievably close at 1,100 yards. Put him astern and moved out to five thousand yards where tracking showed he had changed away also. We then commenced an end around for dawn observation and attack if enemy. Positive enemy identification would have been impossible at night. Shortly after we changed course for our end around his pip at five thousand yards grew smaller and disappeared apparently as he dived. After ranging ahead on his original course, clear of his possible submerged positions, and searching for an hour, proceeded to Nigishima Saki.

As this is the same area in which four torpedoes missed the *Tautog*, it will be interesting to know if any friendly submarine was in this position thirty miles southeast of Kantori Saki. His diving as soon as we reversed course suggests radar, though no interference on SJ or detector was noted.

August 25 (-9)

0220 Dived three thousand yards from Nigishima Saki and moved to within fifteen hundred yards of the beach. Patrol activity started within a half hour, but turned back short of us for some time, probably as a continuous stream of cargo sampans was the only escorting necessary. We did not remain at ease,

0805 however, for on a return sweep down the coast, a PC continued directly on to us. We were two fathoms off the bottom at 275 feet, rigged for silent running, and depth charge too, when he passed directly overhead. He gave no indication of suspecting our presence, and we were able to come to periscope depth as soon as he passed. The repeat performance by the PC, sweeps by a *Nishun Maru* class patrol, and planes on every observation, indicated coming shipping, but they also prevented sufficient observations to fix our position, and we were off Adashika Wan,

1135 a mile down the coast when smoke appeared around Miki Saki.

The top, now visible, developed into a medium mast-funnel-mast and small engine-aft freighter. Guessing they would continue across Adashika Wan, swung left for a stern shot with our last torpedoes. They turned into the narrow bay however, giving us a 130 port truck with a range between 1,500 and 2,000 yards. Confident we could do better, and influenced a little by an escort about to take off our periscope, broke off the attack.

We had been back abreast of our island off Nigishima but

1429 an hour when more smoke came in sight. This proved to be a patrol with a deep throated pinger again sounding like a pile driver on the JK. The JP was too realistic where the noise appeared to scrape and klonk along the bottom. It was almost reassuring when he shifted to short scale on passing 250 feet

1530 above us, and especially so when he commenced driving piles again.

Attacks Nos. 8 & 9

During the next hour, two and then three patrols swept

1715 the area, followed by distant high frequency echo ranging from down the coast. Though its peak was above the range of our receivers, it grew steadily louder until four escort vessels were in sight. The coast was obscured by passing rain, but

1743 soon the enemy ship came in plain sight very close to the beach. She presented a starboard angle, so closed the beach to get on her track before turning off for a stern shot. On the next observation we were on her port bow, so came to the reverse of

1800 her course for low parallax firing.

The enemy was now identified as a modern medium sized diesel tanker, heavily loaded.

She was the identical vessel that slipped by us out of Kazampo on the previous morning. The quarter escort dropped astern as she came on, three others running fanned out on her starboard bow, while a fifth ranged ahead. Our navigator was correct when he tabooed turning for a straight stern shot, and our first echo range, inadvertently taken 180 degrees out, showed 800 yards to the beach. The second, on the enemy, checked with the periscope stadimeter at 600 yards, so using constant

1805 bearings, fired the first Mark 18-1 torpedo at his stern, the second amidships, and the last a third ship length ahead, right for the middle of the three escorts nearly in line of bearing on the starboard bow. Though the depth setting was six feet and gyros around 60 degrees, the first two hit directly as aimed and the third just blew hell out of the leading escort. Though observed sparsely this latter is believed to have been of the *Kushiro Maru* class with standard displacement of about 600 tons.

1808 What was left of the tanker had now sunk and the stern escort was making a run toward where his quarter would have been. Expecting some close ones, put him on our port bow and headed for deep water. The initial barrages permitted high speed and single ping soundings, and in fifteen minutes we reached deep submergence.

The enemy obviously never knew where the torpedoes had come from, and though his search became systematic with a total of sixty-eight depth charges, our 100 turn evasion outflanked him.

2039 With the moon hidden in clouds and the radar detector coupled to the SD antenna, giving only strength two signals on 142, 242, and 306 megacycles, surfaced and cleared the area at full speed. The signal strength decreased rapidly as we withdrew, and searchlights astern disappeared in gathering rain squalls.

August 26 (-9)
0300 In overcast, scuddy weather, continued past Aogashima and set course for Pearl.

September 3 (+9½)
Arrived Pearl.

(C) WEATHER

Normal

(D) TIDAL INFORMATION

West of Omai Saki, a current counter to the Kuroshio was persistently encountered.

(E) NAVIGATIONAL AIDS

In general all navigational lights were burning, but with varying characteristics. In addition, observed fixed dimmed navigational lights which are visible less than three miles.

(F) SHIP CONTACTS

See pages 18 – 19. [p. 109 – 111]

(G) AIRCRAFT CONTACTS

See pages 20 – 23. [111 – 114]

(F) ATTACK DATA

See pages 24 – 42 [115 – 124]

(I) MINES

The possible defensive minefields between Shiono Mitsuki and Ichiye Saki, noted in JICPOA information, is not considered to exist.

(J) ANTI-SUBMARINE MEASURES AND EVASION TACTICS

Speeds up to full under the initial depth charge barrages with soundings taken during explosions facilitated hugging the bottom and clearing the area to deep water. Further evasion at 100 turns for at least two hours invariably left all opposition behind.

(K) MAJOR DEFECTS AND DAMAGE

None.

It is considered that the design of the drum type controller for trim pump, drain pump, turbo-blow, and hydraulic plant, is both poor and antiquated. The unreliability of this controller approaches a major defect in the trim pump installation, where it will not stand up under frequent use and fails repeatedly.

This is essentially the same controller that was installed in U.S.S. *Argonaut* and improved in the *Wahoo* by addition of a stainless steel cover, which had to be left off to make the frequent repairs. It could well be classed with the Model T Ford, and has the same characteristic crank and choke. Its failures are not traceable to inexperienced operators, as it fails as readily for old hands.

Its peak performance occurred on this patrol when its failure put the trim pump out of commission while an enemy sound screen pinged overhead. The silver soldering outfit for convenience is now kept handy by. The following list of failures for this patrol alone help to illustrate the situation,and need for replacement by a Cutler-Hammer type as installed in EB boats:

August 7, 1944   Tripping out. Replaced carbon contacts and
                   loosened metal cover.

August 9, 1944	Tripping out. Reversing the metal cover helped temporarily.
August 10, 1944	Carbon holder broke. Silver soldered holder and renewed carbons.
August 11, 1944	Zero ground. The top of the overload coil was found caked with carbon dust.
August 14, 1944	Tripping out. Adjusted holding coil.
August 17, 1944	Tripping out. Removed metal cover entirely.
August 19, 1944	Tripping out. Tightening loose screws on drum contact and carbon holders.
August 21, 1944	Tripping out. Carbons were found to be making only 10% contact.
August 22, 1944	Carbon holder broke. Silver soldered holder and renewed carbons.
August 26, 1944	Tripping out. Tightened shoes and adjusted carbon contacts.

(L) RADIO

Satisfactory.

(M) RADAR

SD – Not used.
SJ – No interference was noted.

It is believed that the transmitter failures of this particular SJ radar continue to be excessive, compared to other similar units. It is serial number 11, probably constructed under pressure and not up to par. As suggested previously by the Force Electrical Officer, this transmitter should be replaced by another. The part failures for this patrol are listed below.

ITEM	DESCRIPTION	FAILURE REASON
350	Resistor (R45) PPI, 1 meg, 2 watt	Overload due to short.
422	Resistor (R41) PPI, 56,000 ohms	Overload due to short.
426	Resistor (R42) PPI, .1 meg	Overload due to short.
434	Resistor (R43) PPI, .47 meg	Overload due to short.
221	Condenser (C7) Trans. .0068 mfd	Shorted.
111	Resistor (R17) Trans., 10,000 ohms	Low resistance due to age.

291	Resistor (R18) Trans., 68 megs	Low resistance due to age.
434	Resistor (R21) Trans., 47 megs	Low resistance due to age.

No. of FAILURES	FAILURE DESCRIPTION	FAILURE REASON
1	[illegible]	
4	[illegible] tubes	Voltage surge.
2	[illegible]	Old.
2	[illegible] oscillator tube.	Broken
6	[illegible]	Soft.
5	[illegible] tubes	Soft.
2	[illegible]	[illegible]
2	[illegible] tubes	Not known.
2	[illegible]	Poor emission.
1	[illegible] SS tubes	Not known.
1	6X[?] rectifier tube	Loose pin.

The following list of contacts made by the APR-1 equipment is submitted. Although many of these contacts fall in the aircraft radar bands, we were apparently never detected by radar.

Date	Time	Frequency	Pulse Rate	Strength	Position	Probable Location
8-12-44	1135	260 mc	900 cps	1	34-35 N 140-20 E	Nojima Saki
8-12-44	2140	1?0 mc	900 cps	3	3?-35 N 140-40 E	Nojima Saki
8-12-44	?	94 mc	900 cps	3-5	34-35 N 140-20 E	Nojima Saki
8-?-44	?	91 mc	600 cps	5	34-34 N 140-10 E	Nojima Saki
		? mc	600 cps	5		
		? mc	900 cps	2		
		? mc	900 cps	3	34-34 N	
8-?-44	?	? mc	600 cps	2	140-10 E	Nojima Saki (Tokyo Area)
8-?-44	2040	146 mc	600 cps	3	32-21 N 140-33 E	Hachijo Shima
8-?-44	2100	83 mc	600 cps	3	18 mi. SE Kantori Saki	Shiono Misaki
8-?-44	2204	99 mc		2-3	6 mi. SE of Kantori Saki	Shiono Misaki

Date	Time	Frequency	Pulse Rate	Strength	Position	Probable Location
8-20-44	0042	156 mc	900 cps	5	6 mi. SE of Kantori Saki	Ship or Plane
8-20-44		250 mc	900 cps	3-4	33-27 N 136-25 E	Ship or Plane
8-20-44	0000 - 0400	84 mc 99 mc 261 mc	600 cps 900 cps 900 cps	1-5 3 3-4	33-15 N 135-48 E	Shiono Misaki
8-21-44	2030	82 mc 99 mc	900 cps 900 cps	5 2	35-10 N 135-48 E	Shiono Misaki
8-21-44	2330	81 mc	900 cps	2-3	18 mi. from Miki Saki	Shiono Misaki
8-24-44	1930	83 mcs	900 cps	3	33-10 N 135-31 E	Shiono Misaki
8-24-44	2000	99 mcs	600 cps	3	33-11 N 135-55 E	Shiono Misaki
8-24-44	2100	81 mcs	600 cps	5	28 mi. South Shiono Misaki	Shiono Misaki
8-24-44	2350	81 mcs	600 cps	3	6 mi. SW of Miki Saki	Shiono Misaki
8-24-44	2040	142 mcs 242 mcs 306 mcs	600 cps 900 cps 900 cps	2 2 2	22 mi. SW of Miki Saki	Ship or Plane

(N) SOUND GEAR AND SOUND CONDITIONS

Sound conditions were fair. Of interest is the wide frequency range of enemy pinging. It is considered quite probable that many patrols previously considered to be listening only, are actually echo ranging on frequencies higher than can be covered by our receivers. A higher frequency receiver to determine this alone would be valuable.

(O) DENSITY LAYERS

Excellent layers were encountered south of Honshu, generally between 100 and 150 feet.

(P) HEALTH, FOOD, AND HABITABILITY

Good.

(Q) PERSONNEL

(a) Number of men on board during patrol   78
(b) Number of men qualified at start of patrol   47
(c) Number of men qualified at end of patrol   65
(d) Number of unqualified men making their first patrol 8
(e) Number of men advanced in rating during patrol   15

(R) MILES STEAMED, FUEL USED

Midway to Area	2,425 mi.	22,500 gal.
In Area	3,350 mi.	28,000 gal.
Area to Pearl	3,325 mi.	53,000 gal.

(S) DURATION

Days enroute to Area	7
Days in Area	17
Days enroute base	9
Days submerged	12

(T) FACTORS OF ENDURANCE REMAINING

Torpedoes	Fuel	Provision	Personnel
0	7,500	60 days	Indefinite

(U) REMARKS

None

(V) MARK EIGHTEEN TORPEDOES

The routine followed was similar to that of other boats except that it was not found necessary to interchange torpedoes between tubes and rack.

Ship Contacts

No.	Time Date	Lat. Long.	Type	Init. Range	Est. Course	Speed	How Contacted	Remarks
1	0905 8-10-44	34-36 N 137-50 E	Eng. Aft Freighter	12,000	110	9 kts	Periscope	
2	1010 8-10-44	34-35 N 137-35 E	Tanker	8,000	115	9 kts	Periscope	Attack No. 1
3	8-11-44	34-00 N 136-18 E	Eng. Aft Freighter	7,000	180-220	12 kts	Periscope	
4	1355 8-11-44	33-53 N 136-17 E	Medium Tanker	7,000	000-040	10 kts	Periscope	
5	1715 8-11-14	34-12 N 136-19 E	2 Mod. Frs. 2 Escorts	8,000	020	6 kts.	Periscope	Attack Nos. 2 & 3
6	1715 8-12-44	33-42 N 129-16 E	Smoke	20 mi	000	8 kts	Periscope	
7	0654 8-13-44	34-54 N 140-16 E	Medium Freighter	20 mi.	300	12 kts	Periscope	
8	0947 8-20-44	33-37 N 136-01 E	Eng. Aft Fr. 2 Escorts	8,000	215	8 kts	Periscope	Attack No. 4
9	0947 8-20-44	33-22 N 136-37 E	1 Ship 2 Escorts	10,000	100	8 kts	Periscope	
10	1039 8-21-44	33-27 N 135-34 E	1 Eng. Aft Fr. 2 Escorts	8,000	285	8 kts	Periscope	
11	1243 8-21-44	33-30 N 135-29 E	1 Med. Freighter 3 Escorts	8,000	290	8 kts	Periscope	Attack No. 5
12	0033 8-21-44	34-02 N 136-21 E	Gun Boat	6,400	Anchored	0	SJ Radar	Attack No. 6
13	0815 8-23-44	34-36 N 137-50 E	3 Freighters 3 Escorts	10,000	280	9 kts	Periscope	
14	0923 8-23-44	34-37 N 137-50 E	Old Type DD	8,000	Various	15 kts	Periscope	
15	1017 8-23-44	34-37 N 137-50 E	Naval Trans. 4 Escorts	13,000	095	8 kts	Periscope	Attack No. 7
16	0952 8-24-44	33-30 N 135-21 E	Diesel Tanker 1 Escort	12,000	093	9 kts	Periscope	
17	1225 8-24-44	33-30 N 135-22 E	2 Freighters 7 Escorts	12,000	315	10 kts	Periscope	
18	2342 8-24-44	33-40 N 136-16 E	Submarine	1,100	145	12 kts	Sight	
19	1135 8-25-44	33-54 N 136-16 E	2 Freighters	4,800	015	8 kts	Periscope	
20	1743 8-25-44	33-55 N 136-18 E	1 Diesel Tanker 5 Escorts	8,000	033	8 kts	Periscope	Attacks No. 8 & 9

Small Craft Contacts

No.	Time Date	Lat. Long.	Type	Init. Range	Est. Course	Speed	How Contacted	Remarks
1	0457 8-10-44	34-36 N 134-47 E	PC Boat 2 masts	12,000	Various	12 kts	Periscope	
2	0935 8-10-44	34-35 N 137-47 E	Patrol	6,000	Various	12 kts	Periscope	
3	0745 8-11-44	33-46 N 136-19 E	Patrol	7,000	Various	10 kts	Periscope	
4	0853 8-11-44	33-57 N 136-19 E	Fishing Boat	5,000	160	7 kts	Periscope	
5	0736 8-12-44	33-43 N 139-32 E	Patrol	6,000	Various	7 kts	Periscope	
6	1135 8-12-44	33-45 N 139-48 E	Patrol	6,000	090	6 kts	Periscope	
7	1505 8-12-44	33-47 N 139-54 E	Patrol	6,000	Various	8 kts	Periscope	
8	0717 8-13-44	34-59 N 144-23 E	Sampans Patrol	8,000	Various	6 kts	Periscope	
9	1028 8-13-44	34-56 N 140-20 E	Fishing Patrol	12,000	280	6 kts	Periscope	
10	1133 8-13-44	34-56 N 140-20 E	Sampans Patrols	8,000	Various 240	6 kts	Periscope	
11	1400 8-13-44	34-58 N 140-22 E	Fishing Boat	10,000	293	5 kts	Periscope	
12	0424 8-14-44	33-50 N 140-36 E	Patrol Yacht	8,000	Various	Various	Periscope	Gun Attack No. 1
13	0450 8-20-44	33-50 N 136-10 E	Sampan Fishing	10,000	Stopped	5 kts	Periscope	
14	0500 8-20-44	33-50 N 136-10 E	Fishing Sampan (2)	15,000	Stopped	5 kts	Periscope	
15	0730 8-23-44	34-35 N 137-50 E	Sailboat	15,000	320	4 kts	Periscope	
16	0923 8-23-44	34-37 N 137-50 E	PC Boat	800	270	6 kts	Periscope	
17	0952 8-24-44	33-30 N 135-21 E	2 Patrol Boats	8,000	355	10 kts	Periscope	
18	1020 8-24-44	33-30 N 135-21 E	Trawler	2,300	265	8 kts	Periscope	
19	8-25-44	33-54 N 136-13 E	Patrols	4,000	Various	6 kts	Periscope	
20	1002 8-25-44	33-54 N 136-13 E	Sampans	Various	Various	5 kts	Periscope	

No.	Time Date	Lat. Long.	Type	Init. Range	Est. Course	Speed	How Contacted	Remarks
21	1425 8-25-44	33-54 N 136-13 E	2 Patrols	10,000	050	8 kts	Periscope	
22	1530 8-25-44	33-54 N 136-13 E	2 Fishing Boat 2 Patrols	5,000	Various	6 kts	Periscope	

Aircraft Contacts (Revised)

	Contact Number	1	2	3	4	5	6	7
S	Date	8-8-44	8-8-44	8-10-44	8-10-44	8-11-44	8-12-44	8-12-44
U	Zone Time	0950	1410	0850	1025	1914	1006	1355
B	Lat	33-32 N	32-30 N	34-30 N	34-33 N	33-42 N	32-50 N	32-51 N
M	Long	142-15 E	141-10 E	137-50 E	137-55 E	136-28 E	129-50 E	139-42 E
A	Speed	3½	11	3	3	2	3	3
R	Course	273	273	000	050	140	090	240
I	Trim	Surf	Surf	Per	Per	Per	Per	Per
N	Time Since	No	No	No	No	No	No	No
E	SD Search	Search	Search	Search	Search	Search	Search	Search

	Number	1	1	1	1	1	1	1
A			2 Eng.	2 Eng.	2 Eng.		2 Eng.	
I	Type	Betty	Bomber	Bomber	Bomber	Float	Bomber	Lily
R	Prob							
C	Mission	Pat.	Pat.	Esc.	Esc.	H.	Pat.	Pat.
R	Contacted							
A	by:	Lookout	Sight	Per.	Per.	Per.	Per.	Per.
F	I.R.	8 mi.	10 mi.	6 mi.	4 mi.	4 mi.	12 mi.	16 mi.
T	Elev. Angle	10	8	3	10	4	10	4
	Detected?	ND	ND	ND	ND	ND	ND	ND

			1	2	3	4	5	6	7
C		{State	3	3	2	2	1	1	1
O		{							
N	Sea	{ Br.	012	350	246	196	029	090	090
D		{							
I	Visibility		30	30	20	20	10	20	Over 30
T		{Ht	20,000	20,000	15,000	15,000	20,000	10,000	25,000
I	Clouds	{							
O		{%	.8	.5	.4	.4	.1	.6	.3
N		{overcast							
S	Moon:		Daytime	Daytime	Daytime	Daytime	Daytime	Daytime	Daytime

Type of S/M Camouflage on this patrol <u>Light Gray</u>

Contact Number		8	9	10	11	12	13	14
S U B M A R I N E	Date	8-12-44	8-13-44	8-13-44	8-13-44	8-13-44	8-14-44	8-14-44
	Zone Time	1622	0935	1140	1417	1620	1002	1455
	Lat	33-46 N	34-53 N	34-45 N	35-01 N	35-04 N	33-41 N	33-36 N
	Long	139-30 E	140-12 E	140-22 E	140-51 E	140-50 E	140-27 E	140-32 E
	Speed	2	3	2	2	2	4	4
	Course	320	290	200	030	230	000	340
	Trim	Per.	Per.	Per.	Per.	Per.	Per.	Per.
	Time Since SD Search	No Search	No Search	No Search	No Search	No Search	No Search	No Search
A I R C R A F T	Number	1	4	2	1	2	1	1
	Type	—	2 Eng. Bomber	2 Eng. Bomber	Betty	Bomb	—	Bomb
	Prob Mission	Pat.	Esc.	Pat.	Pat.	Pat.	Pat.	Pat.
	Contacted by:	Per.	Per.	Per.	Per.	Per.	Per.	Per.
	I.R.	10 mi.	6 mi.	15 mi.	16 mi.	15 mi.	15 mi.	8 mi.
	Elev. Angle	—	1	4	4	4	4	8
	Detected?	ND	ND	ND	ND	ND	ND	ND
C O N D I T I O N S	Sea {State	1	1	3	2	2	1	2
	Sea { Br.	—	260	350				
	Visibility	—	Over 30	30	25	20	Over 30	25
	Clouds {Ht	—	15,000	16,000	9,000	6,000	10,000	7,000
	{% overcast	—	.4	.4	.2	.1	.5	.3
	Moon:	Day	Day	Day	Day	Day	Day	Day

Type of S/M Camouflage this patrol: <u>Light Gray</u>

Contact Number		15	16	17	18	19	20	21
S U B M A R I N E	Date	8-14-44	8-16-44	8-17-44	8-17-44	8-18-44	8-20-44	8-21-44
	Zone Time	2325	1350	0725	1326	1310	1717	0910
	Lat	33-40 N	32-27 N	32-05 N	31-45 N	32-05 N	33-55 N	33-20 N
	Long	140-36 E	143-03 E	143-50 E	144-05 E	143-20 E	136-30 E	135-39 E
	Speed	18	19	10	12	17	2	2
	Course	160	027	189	201	277	090	305
	Trim	Surf.	Surf.	Surf.	Surf.	Surf.	Per.	Per.
	Minutes Since Last SD Search	No Search	No Search	SD Manned	SD Manned	SD Manned	No Search	No Search
A I R C R A F T	Number	1	1	1	1	1	1	1
	Type	—	Mavis			Mavis	Dave	Float
	Prob Mission	Pat.	Pat.	Pat.	Pat.	Pat.	H.	Pat.
	Contacted by:	Lookout	Lookout	Lookout	Per	Lookout	Per.	Per.
	I.R.	—	5 mi.	15 mi.	20 mi.	10 mi.	5 mi.	12 mi.
	Elev. Angle	—	20	4	4	3	10	4
	Range & Relative Bearing of Plane When it Detected S/M	ND	6 mi. 135	ND	ND	ND	4 mi. 155	ND
C O N D I T I O N S	Sea {State	1	3	1	2	2	2	2
	Sea { Br.	—	015	050	292	030	030	045
	Visibility	2	30	30	Over 30	Over 30	15	12
	Clouds {Ht	5,000	15,000	4,000	20,000	15,000	10,000	10,000
	{% overcast	.2	.4	.1	.2	.3	.8	.1
	Moon:	None	Day	Day	Day	Day	Day	Day

Type of S/M Camouflage this patrol: <u>Light Gray</u>

Contact Number		22	23	24	25	26	27	28
S U B M A R I N E	Date	8-23-44	8-23-44	8-23-44	8-23-44	8-23-44	8-25-44	8-25-44
	Zone Time	0615	0710	0730	1010	1015	1025	1110
	Lat	34-35 N	34-35 N	34-35 N	34-27 N	34-37 N	33-54 N	33-54 N
	Long	137-50 E	137-50 E	137-50 E	137-49 E	137-40 E	136-13 E	136-13 E
	Speed	2	2	2	2	2	2	2
	Course	000(T)	322(T)	322(T)	090	090	040	200
	Trim	Per.	Per.	Per.	Per.	Per.	Per.	Per.
	Minutes Since Last SD Search	—	—	—	—	—	—	—
A I R C R A F T	Number	1	1	3	4	1	1	2
	Type	Dave	Kate	Kate	Nell	Nell	Dave	Bombers
	Prob Mission	Pat.	T.	Pat.	T.	T.	Pat.	Pat.
	Contacted by:	Per.	Per.	Per.	Per.	Per.	Per.	Per.
	I.R.	10 mi.	6 mi.	6 mi.	7 mi.	7 mi.	4 mi.	10 mi.
	Elev. Angle	3°	5°	5°	3°	3°	15°	3°
	Range & Relative Bearing of Plane When it Detected S/M	ND	ND	ND	ND	ND	ND	ND
C O N D I T I O N S	Sea {State	3	3	3	3	3	3	3
	Sea { Br.	090	090	090	090	090	140	140
	Visibility	12 mi.	12 mi.	12 mi.	12 mi.	12 mi.	12 mi.	12 mi.
	Clouds {Ht	3,000	3,000	3,000	3,000	3,000	3,000	3,000
	{% overcast	7	6	5	5	5	4	4
	Moon:	Day	Day	Day	Day	Day	Day	Day

Type of S/M Camouflage this patrol: <u>Light Gray</u>

U.S.S. *Tang* (SS 306)	Torpedo Attack No. 1	Patrol No. Four
Time: 1010 (-9)	Date: 8-10-44	Lat: 34-34 N
		Long: 137-35 E

TARGET DATA – DAMAGE INFLICTED

Description of Target: 1 Medium Tanker, 5,000 tons.
Ship Sunk: None.
Target Data: Draft: 20' Course: 115 Speed: 9 Range: 1,200
Own Data: Course: 050 Speed: 3 Depth: 63' Angle: 0
Type Attack: Day Submerged.

FIRE CONTROL AND TORPEDO DATA #1

Tube No.	1	2	3
Track Angle	108 S	112 S	114 S
Gyro Angle	355	359	001
Depth Set	6'	6'	6'
Hit or Miss	Miss	Miss	Miss
Erratic	No	No	No
Mk. Torpedo	23	23	23
Serial No.	61832	41159	49363
Mk. Exploder	6 - 4	6 - 4	6 - 4
Serial No.	7769	3288	8341
Actuation	—	—	—
Mk. Warhead	16 - 1	16 - 1	16 -1
Serial No.	11304	9455	12191
Explosive	TPX	TPX	TPX
Firing Interval	13 Sec.	10 Sec.	
Type Spread	Divergent point of aim.		
Sea Condition	Flat calm		
Overhaul Activity	Midway		

U.S.S. *Tang* (SS 306)   Torpedo Attack No. 2   Patrol No. Four
Time: 1715 (-9)   Date: 8-11-44   Lat: 34-12 N
                                               Long: 136-19 E

TARGET DATA – DAMAGE INFLICTED

Description of Target: 1 Medium freighter, *Biyo Maru* class,
                         (EC) 5,425 tons.
Ship Sunk: 1 Medium freighter, 5,425 tons.
Damage Determined by: Observed one torpedo hit, breaking ship in two.
Target Data: Draft: 26' Course: 020 Speed: 6 Range: 1,800
Own Data: Course: 090 Speed: 2   Depth: 64' Angle: ½° Dive.
Type Attack: Day Submerged.

FIRE CONTROL AND TORPEDO DATA #2

Tube No.	1	2	3
Track Angle	100 S	102 S	104 S
Gyro Angle	012	013	015
Depth Set	6'	6'	6'
Hit or Miss	Hit	Miss	Miss
Erratic	No	No	No
Mk. Torpedo	23	23	23
Serial No.	49437	61741	61764
Mk. Exploder	6 - 4	6 - 4	6 - 4
Serial No.	933	17938	2158
Actuation	Contact	—	—
Mk. Warhead	16 - 1	16 - 1	16 - 1
Serial No.	13055	12773	12828
Explosive	TPX	TPX	TPX
Firing Interval	8 Sec.	8 Sec.	
Type Spread	Divergent point of aim.		
Sea Conditions	Flat calm		
Overhaul Activity	Midway		

U.S.S. *Tang* (SS 306)	Torpedo Attack No. 3	Patrol No. Four
Time: 1715 (-9)	Date: 8-11-44	Lat: 34-12 N
		Long: 136-19 E

TARGET DATA – DAMAGE INFLICTED

Description of Target: 1 Medium freighter, *Akasi Maru* class,
(EU) 3,057 – 3,461 tons.
Ship Damaged: 1 Medium Freighter, 4,000 tons.
Damage Determined by: Recorded two timed hits and heard characteristic breaking up noises on last observed target bearing.
Target Data: Draft: 20' Course: 020   Speed: 6   Range: 1,500
Own Data: Course: 290 Speed: 2   Depth: 64'   Angle: ½° Rise
Type: Day Submerged.

FIRE CONTROL AND TORPEDO DATA #3

Tube No.	4	5	6
Track Angle	91 S	90 S	90 S
Gyro Angle	002	000	001
Depth Set	6'	6'	6'
Hit or Miss	Hit	Hit	Miss
Mk. Torpedo	23	23	23
Serial No.	61680	53013	41561
Mk. Exploder	6 - 4	6 - 4	6 - 4
Serial No.	1542	343	7162
Actuation	Contact	Contact	—
Mk. Warhead	16 - 1	16 - 1	16 - 1
Serial No.	13863	13082	12900
Explosive	TPX	TPX	TPX
Firing Interval	8 Sec.	8 Sec.	
Type Spread:	Divergent point of aim.		
Sea Conditons	Flat calm.		
Overhaul Activity	Midway		

U.S.S. *Tang* (SS 306)   Torpedo Attack No. 4   Patrol No. Four
Time: 1108 (-9)   Date: 8-20-44   Lat: 33-37 N
                                                        Long: 136-01 E

[TARGET DATA – DAMAGE INFLICTED]

Description of Target: Medium freighter, engines aft.
Ship Sunk: None
Target Data: Draft: 18' Course: 218   Speed: 8   Range: 900
Own Data: Course: 309 Speed: 3   Depth: 64' Angle: 0
Type Attack: Day submerged.

FIRE CONTROL AND TORPEDO DATA #4

Tube No.	5	6
Track Angle	118 P	128 P
Gyro Angle	332	322
Depth Set	6'	6'
Hit or Miss	Miss	Miss
Erratic	No	*Yes
Mk. Torpedo	23	23
Serial No.	52826	52840
Mk. Exploder	6 - 4	6 - 4
Serial No.	17860	2471
Actuation	—	—
Mk. Warhead	16 - 1	16 - 1
Serial No.	13170	3500
Explosive	TPX	TPX
Firing Interval	10 sec.	
Type Spread	Divergent point of aim.	
Sea Conditions	Flat calm	
Overhaul Activity	Midway	

*Torpedo did not run.

U.S.S. *Tang* (SS 306)   Torpedo Attack No. 5   Patrol No. Four
Time: 1317 (-9)   Date: 8-21-44   Lat: 33-30 N
                                          Long: 135-29 E

TARGET DATA – DAMAGE INFLICTED

Description of Target: Medium freighter
Ship Sunk: None.
Target Data: Draft: 15'   Course: 290   Speed: 8   Range: 1,650
Own Data: Course: 205   Speed: 3   Depth: 64'   Angle: 0
Type Attack: Day submerged.

FIRE CONTROL AND TORPEDO DATA #5

Tube No.	7	8	9
Track Angle	104 P	107 P	106 P
Gyro Angle	161	158	160
Depth Set	6'	6'	6'
Hit or Miss	Miss	Miss	Miss
Erratic	No	No	No
Mk. Torpedo	18 - 1	18 - 1	18 - 1
Serial No.	54308	54311	54508
Mk. Exploder	8 - 5	8 - 5	8 - 5
Serial No.	8093	8330	8406
Actuation	—	—	—
Mk. Warhead	18 - 1	18 - 1	18 - 1
Serial No.	2209	2184	2249
Explosive	TPX	TPX	TPX
Firing Interval	9 sec.	14 sec.	
Type Spread	Divergent point of aim.		
Sea Conditions	Flat calm.		
Overhaul Activity	Midway		

U.S.S. *Tang* (SS 306)   Torpedo Attack No. 6   Patrol No. Four
Time: 0142 (-9)   Date: 8-22-44   Lat: 34-02 N
                                                        Long: 136-21 E

TARGET DATA – DAMAGE INFLICTED

Description of Target: 1 Patrol Gun Boat, 1,500 tons standard displacement.
Ship Sunk: Patrol Gun Boat, 1,500 tons.
Damage Determined by: Observed ship blow up.
Target Data: Draft: 6' *Course: 150   Speed: 0   Range: 950
Own Data: Course: 060 - 240   Speed: 0 - 0   Depth: Surf.   Angle: 0
Type Attack: Night surface
        *Anchored.

FIRE CONTROL AND TORPEDO DATA #6

Tube No.	7	8	5	6
Track Angle	90 P	90 P	90 P	90 P
Gyro Angle	176	172	358	001
Depth Set	3'	3'	0	0
Hit or Miss	Miss	Miss	Miss	Hit
Erratic	*Yes	*Yes	*Yes	No
Mk. Torpedo	18 - 1	18 - 1	23	23
Serial No.	54396	53736	41253	41664
Mk. Exploder	8 - 5	8 - 5	6 - 5	6 - 4
Serial No.	8244	8309	6217	8026
Actuation	—	—	—	Contact
Mk. Warhead	18	18 - 1	16 - 1	16
Serial No.	2328	2189	11316	17214
Explosive	TPX	TPX	TPX	TPX
Firing Interval	1 Min. 32 Sec. 14 Min. 20 Sec 1 Min. 35 sec.			
Type Spread	Single shots			
Sea Conditions	Flat calm.			
Overhaul Activity	Midway			

    *7   Sinker hit bottom after 500 Yd. run.
    *8   Phosporescent wake barely discernable
         apparently ran deep.
    *5   Took 30 Yd. jog to left before settling on course.

U.S.S. *Tang* (SS 306)	Torpedo Attack No. 7	Patrol No. Four
Time: 1118 (-9)	Date: 8-23-44	Lat: 34-37 N
		Long: 137-50 E

TARGET DATA – DAMAGE INFLICTED

Description of Target: Large Naval Transport
Ship Sunk: Large Naval Transport.
              Gross Tonnage about 10,000
              Estimated standard displacement 15,000.
Damage Determined by: Observed two hits and enemy sink.
Target Data: Draft: 26' Course: 095 Speed: 8½ Range: 800
Own Ship: Course: 358 Speed: 3 Depth: 64' Angle: 0
Type Attack: Day submerged.

FIRE CONTROL AND TORPEDO DATA #7

Tube No.	1	2	3
Track Angle	108 S	108 S	110 S
Gyro Angle	023	027	029
Depth Set	6'	6'	6'
Hit or Miss	Hit	Miss	Hit
Erratic	No	No	No
Mk. Torpedo	23	23	23
Serial No.	52992	61757	41054
Mk. Exploder	6 - 4	6 - 4	6 - 4
Serial No.	7511	8079	7362
Actuation	Contact	—	Contact
Mk. Warhead	16 - 1	16 - 1	16 - 1
Serial No.	14014	17188	12889
Explosive	TPX	TPX	TPX
Firing Interval	9 sec.	11 sec.	
Type Spread	Divergent point of aim		
Sea Conditions	Flat calm		
Overhaul Activity	Midway		

U.S.S. *Tang* (SS 306)   Torpedo Attack No. 8   Patrol No. Four
Time: 1805 (-9)   Date: 8-25-44   Lat: 33-55 N
    Long.   136-18 E

TARGET DATA – DAMAGE INFLICTED

Description of Target: 1 Medium Diesel Tanker, 5,000 tons.
Ship Sunk: 1 Medium Diesel Tanker, 5,000 tons.
Damage Determined by: Observed two hits disintegrate ship and pieces sink.
Target Data: Draft: 24' Course: 033   Speed: 8   Range: 600
Own Data: Course: 225   Speed: 3   Depth: 64' Angle: 0
Type Attack: Day submerged.

FIRE CONTROL AND TORPEDO DATA #8

Tube No.	7	8
Track Angle	103 P	110 P
Gyro Angle	245	238
Depth Set	6'	6'
Hit or Miss	Hit	Hit
Erratic	No	No
Mk. Torpedo	18 - 1	18 -1
Serial No.	54760	54546
Mk. Exploder	8 - 5	8 - 5
Serial No.	8516	8315
Actuation	Contact	Contact
Mk. Warhead	18	18 - 1
Serial No.	2141	2361
Explosive	TPX	TPX
Firing Interval	10 Sec.	
Type Spread	Divergent point of aim.	
Sea Conditions	Flat calm	
Overhaul Activity	Midway	

U.S.S. *Tang* (SS 306)   Torpedo Attack No. 9   Patrol No. Four
Time: 1805 (-9)   Date: 8-25-44   Lat: 33-55 N
                              Long: 136-18 E

TARGET DATA – DAMAGE INFLICTED

Description of Target: Three Patrol vessels on line of bearing
Ship Sunk: *Kushiro Maru* class escort vessel (PCE), (EU), 600 tons
            standard displacement.
Damage Determined by: Observed torpedo explosion blow ship to pieces.
Target Data: Draft: 8'   Course: 033   Speed: 8   Range: 1,800
Own Data: Course: 225   Speed: 3   Depth: 64'   Angle: 0
Type Attack: Day submerged.

FIRE CONTROL AND TORPEDO DATA #9

Tube No.	9
Track Angle	116 P
Gyro Angle	230
Depth Set	6'
Hit or Miss	Hit
Erratic	No
Mk. Torpedo	18 - 1
Serial No.	54685
Mk. Exploder	8 - 5
Serial No.	8,500
Actuation	Contact
Mk. Warhead	18
Serial No.	2201
Explosive	TPX
Sea Conditions	Flat calm
Overhaul Activity	Midway

U.S.S. *Tang* (SS 306)   Gun Attack No. 1   Patrol No. Four
Time: 1832 (-9)   Date: 8-14-44   Lat: 33-03 N
                                                          Long: 140-35 E

TARGET DATA – DAMAGE INFLICTED

Damaged: Patrol Yacht
Damage Determined by: Observed hits

DETAILS OF ACTION

Type gun used: 4"/50 cal.
Ammunition expended: 60 rounds of H.E.
                        28 rounds of Common
Effectiveness of fire: Eight sure hits
Average range: 4,500 to 7,000

FB5-43/A16-3   Submarine Division Forty Three

Serial (0117)   Care of Fleet Post Office,
                                                 San Francisco, California,
<u>CONFIDENTIAL</u>   5 September 1944.

<u>First Endorsement to</u>
U.S.S. *Tang* conf.
ltr. A16-3, Serial 013
of 3 September 1944.

From: The Commander Submarine Division Forty Three.
To: The Commander-in-Chief, United States Fleet.
Via: (A) The Commander Submarine Squadron Four.
          (B) The Commander Submarine Force, Pacific Fleet
          (C) The Commander-in-Chief, U.S. Pacific Fleet.

Subject: U.S.S. *Tang* (SS306), Report of Fourth War Patrol,
          Comments on.

    1.   The Fourth War Patrol of the U.S.S. *Tang* was of thirty days' duration, seventeen of which were spent in the assigned areas. The report is excellently witten and should be of great value to submarines which patrol this difficult area, the coastal waters of Japan. The courses of action taken, the reasons therefor, and general conduct of this patrol reveal submarine operations of the highest order.

<u>Torpedo Attack No. 1 Daylight, Submerged</u>
<u>10 August 1944</u>

    Three torpedoes fired at a tanker at 1,100 yards' range and with excellent firing data resulted in no hits and no explosions on the beach 3,000 yards away. With depth of water of only eight feet, it is possible that initial dive of Mk. 23 torpedoes caused them to strike bottom.

<u>Torpedo Attack No. 2 & No. 3 Daylight, Submerged</u>
<u>11 August 1944</u>

    Position was attained 1,700 yards on the beam of two freighters in column accompanied by a gunboat and a smaller escort. Three torpedoes were fired at the first ship and a similar salvo at the second ship. After a quick look showed the gunboat proceeding rapidly and closely across the stern, one hit was observed amidships in the first target, resulting in a disintegrating explosion. Two timed hits were heard in the second target as *Tang* took evasive action. The counter-attack is described as "tooth-shaking."

Gun Attack No. 1 – 14 August 1944

A patrol yacht was attacked with four-inch gun. Twenty MM fire was returned, forcing *Tang* to keep range greater than 4,500 yards. Eight hits were made, demolishing the deck house aft and exploding in his side and upper works.

Torpedo Attack No. 4, Daylight Submerged
20 August 1944

Of two torpedoes fired at a medium freighter, one missed astern and the other didn't run.

Torpedo Attack No. 5, Daylight Submerged
21 August 1944

No hits were obtained when three Mk. 18 torpedoes were fired at a medium freighter at 1,650 yards range. Deep running of torpedoes is considered most probable cause for misses.

Torpedo Attack No. 6, Night Surface
22 August 1944

A patrol vessel of about 1,500 tons was found at anchor in 20 fathoms of water; the night was black. This vessel was recognized as one which had previously depth charged *Tang*. Two Mk. 18 torpedoes from stern tubes produced no results so bow tubes were brought to bear and two Mk. 23's fired. The first took a jog to the left and missed astern, but the second hit the point of aim and the target sank after a spectacular explosion.

Torpedo Attack No. 7, Daylight Submerged
23 August 1944

Shortly after a sweep by A/S vessels and aircraft a large transport accompanied by a PC or DE ahead, an SC on his bow, and an LST and PC astern, was sighted. A beautiful approach put *Tang* in position 800 yards abeam and three

Mk. 23 torpedoes were fired on a 105° track. Two hits resulted in the sinking of this valuable loaded transport.

Torpedo Attacks No. 8 & No. 9, Daylight Submerged
25 August 1944

From a position inshore of a modern medium diesel tanker proceeding close to the beach, three Mk. 18 torpedoes were fired. Small parallax shots were necessary, for *Tang* couldn't turn toward beach, distance 800 yards, for straight stern shots. Two hits sank the tanker and the third torpedo sank one of the escorts.

2.   Faulty torpedo performance appears to have prevented bringing back an even fuller bag.

3.   The well-worded indictment of the drum-type controller for the trim pump verifies the need for replacement of this equipment.

4.   *Tang* returned in excellent condition, and refit will be accomplished in normal period.

5.   The Commanding Officer, officers and crew are heartily congratulated on the completion of another highly successful patrol. It is recommended that the following damage to the enemy be credited.

Sunk

1 Medium Freighter, *Biyo Maru* Class	5,500 tons EC
1 Medium Freighter, *Akasi Maru* Class	3,461 tons EU
1 Patrol Gun Boat	1,500 tons EU
1 Large Naval Transport	15,000 tons EU
1 Medium Diesel Tanker	5,000 tons EU
1 Escort, *Kushiro Maru* Class	600 tons EU
Total	30,000 tons.

Damaged

1 Patrol Yacht

D.C. White
Submarine Squadron Four   11/tel

FC5-4/A16-3

Fleet Post Office,
San Francisco, California,
11 September 1944.

Serial 0345

CONFIDENTIAL

Second Endorsement to:
U.S.S. *Tang* report of
Fourth War Patrol.

From: The Commander Submarine Squadron Four.
To: The Commander-in-Chief, United States Fleet.
Via: (1) The Commander Submarine Force, Pacific Fleet.
             (2) The Commander-in-Chief, U.S Pacific Fleet.

Subject: U.S.S. *Tang* – Report of Fourth War Patrol.

1.   Forwarded, concurring in the remarks of Commander Submarine Division Forty-Three, and with particular emphasis on paragraph three (3).

2.   The evasion tactics employed by the Commanding Officer of the *Tang* (paragraph J), allowed penetration of shoal water for attacks on coast-wise and anchored shipping with excellent results. As the wide open sea areas diminish by reason of further U.S. Naval conquest, it is incumbent upon all submariners to develop the tactics of attack and evasion in shoal water. The tactics used in this patrol point the way. The Commanding Officer stated verbally that in his opinion enemy vessels hugging the coast were cramped in their zig-zag tactics, and therefore resorted to frequent changes of speed.

3.   The intelligence data gathered and presented in this report is a model of lucidity.

4.   Again, it is the pleasure of Commander Submarine Squadron Four to congratulate this outstanding ship on an outstanding performance against the enemy.

C.F. Krok
Submarine Force, Pacific Fleet   hch

U.S.S. *Tang* (SS-306)

FF12-10/A16-3(15)/(18)

Serial 01980

CONFIDENTIAL

Care of Fleet Post Office,
San Francisco, California
15 September 1944

Third Endorsement to
Tang Report of
Fourth War Patrol

Note: This report will be
destroyed prior to
entering patrol area.

ComSubPac Patrol Report No. 522.
U.S.S. *Tang* – Fourth War Patrol

From:	The Commander Submarine Force, Pacific Fleet.
To:	The Commander-in-Chief, United States Fleet.
Via:	The Commander-in-Chief, U.S. Pacific Fleet.

Subject: U.S.S. *Tang* (SS306) – Report of Fourth War Patrol.
(31 July to 3 September 1944).

1. The fourth war patrol of the *Tang* was conducted off the Coast of Honshu in the Japanese Empire waters.
2. The *Tang*, continuing her illustrious record, closed the coastline and sought out enemy traffic with daring and skill. She encountered first rate enemy anti-submarine forces and underwent intense depth charging. Due to expert evasion tactics, however, she avoided any serious damage and made nine aggressive attacks on the elusive coastal traffic.
3. This patrol is designated as "Successful" for Combat Insignia Award.
4. The Commander Submarine Force, Pacific Fleet, congratulates the commanding officer, officers, and crew on this fourth consecutive, aggressive, and highly successful patrol. During these four patrols the *Tang* has built up the outstanding record of 18 ships sunk and a total tonnage of 122,469 tons, and one 4,000 ton ship damaged in addition to having rescued 22 downed aviators and damaged one small craft by gun fire. The *Tang* is credited with having inflicted the following damage upon the enemy during this patrol:

Sunk

1 – Medium AK (*Biyo Maru* Type) (EC)	–	5,400 tons	(Attack No. 2)
1 – Patrol Gun Boat (EU)	–	1,500 tons	(Attack No. 6)
1 – Large Naval Transport (EU)	–	10,000 tons	(Attack No. 7)

1 – Medium AO (EU)	–	5,000 tons	(Attack No. 8)
1 – Escort Vessel (*Kushino Maru* type) (EU)	–	600 tons	(Attack No. 9)

Total Sunk	22,500 tons

Damaged

1 – Medium AK (*Akasi Maru* Type) (EU)	–	4,000 tons	(Attack No. 3)
1 – [PY] (EU)	–	100 tons	(Gun Attack No. 1)

Total Damaged	4,100 tons
Total Sunk and Damaged	26,600 tons

Distribution:
(Complete Reports)

Cominch	(7)	C.A. Lockwood
CNO	(5)	
CinCpac	(6)	
Intel.Cen.Pac.Ocean Areas	(1)	
ComServPac	(1)	
CinClant	(1)	
ComSubLant	(8)	
S/M School, NL	(2)	
ComSoPac	(2)	
ComSoWesPac	(1)	
ComSubSoWesPac	(2)	
CTF 72	(2)	
ComNorPac	(1)	
ComSubsPac	(40)	
SUBAD, MI	(2)	
ComSubsPacSubOrdCom	(3)	
All Squadron and Division Commanders, Pacific	(2)	
SubsTrainPac	(2)	
All Submarines, Pacific	(1)	

E.L. Hymes, 2nd,
Flag Secretary.

Patrol Five, 24 September 1944 – 25 October 1944

SS306/A16-3 U.S.S. Tang (SS306) rch

Care of Fleet Post Office,
San Francisco, California,
19 September 1945.

CONFIDENTIAL

From: The Commanding Officer.
To: The Commander in Chief, United States Fleet.
Via: (1) The Commander Submarine Force, Pacific Fleet.
             (2) The Commander in Chief, U.S. Pacific Fleet.

Subject: U.S.S. *Tang* (SS306) – Report of War Patrol Five.

Enclosure: (A) Subject Report.

1. Enclosure (A), covering the Fifth War Patrol of this vessel conducted in the Formosa Strait during the period 24 September 1944 to 25 October 1944 and a report of her loss is forwarded herewith.

R.H. O'Kane

(A) PROLOGUE

Returned from 4th Patrol on 3 September, 1944 and conducted patrol refit at the U.S. Submarine Base, Pearl Harbor, T.H. In order to take part in the coming Formosa raid and to be in a position inside the Formosa Straits to intercept Japanese reinforcements for the coming Philippine Campaign, training and loading were completed four days in advance of schedule. Loaded 24 Mark 18 Mod 1 torpedoes already prepared for the U.S.S. *Tambor*, who had been delayed.

(B) NARRATIVE

24 September 1944
1300 Departed for Formosa Strait via Midway, proceeding at full power to this last fueling base.

27 September 1944
0700 Moored at Submarine Base, Midway and received their usual good welcome and services. With fuel in every available corner, departed at noon for our patrol area. Proceeding at two engine speed.

27 September – 5 October 1944
(East Latitude Date)
Routine training enroute to station showed gratifying results. Received information that the *Trigger – Sunfish*[1] pack were looking for a small Jap ship whose last reported position plotted directly on our track. We were apparently ahead of those boats which had left Pearl a few hours ahead of us and had proceeded via Saipan, so felt we stood a good chance of finding him first.

6 October 1944
Ran into threatening weather which quickly developed into a full-fledged typhoon. Continued on the surface still in hope of intercepting the ships, but soon found ourselves on the inside semi-circle, with seas and wind which would prohibit any sort of attack if he were located. The barometer dropped to 27.80, the waves broke over the raised periscope, and even had small waves on their backs. It was a sight such as none of us had witnessed before. Needless to say, our bridge watch had been secured and the ship closed up, running on the

---

[1]   *Clear the Bridge!* gives the second submarine as *Silversides* instead of *Sunfish*, and *Trigger's* tenth war patrol report indicated she was proceeding in company with *Silversides* and *Salmon* at this time.

battery. It was frankly considered too late to dive as we often hung at 60° by the bubble inclinometer in the control room. What the momentary extra loss of stability on diving, especially if the ballast tanks flooded unevenly, would have brought about is still a question in our minds.

7 October 1944

Having worked through to the safe side and with slowly moderating sea, proceeded toward Formosa Straits. Our first fix showed us having been set 60 miles in a direction opposite to that which we steered while pulling clear of the storm.

8 October – 9 October 1944

As the sea permitted went to three-engine speed. Dived for one plane which we are quite sure could flap its wings however.

10 October 1944

With the mountains of Formosa in view dead ahead from moon on and the top of Yonakuni Shima rising on our starboard hand, went to four-engine speed so as to pass into the Strait shortly after dark. About 2100 made contact with and tracked a small craft which turned out to be a patrol vessel when observed from 8,000 yards. Put him astern and continued on past Kirun around the northern tip of Formosa inside Kahei Sho and into our area.

11 October 1944
Attack No. 1

0400 When about four miles west of Puki Kaku made radar contact at 17,000 yards on a ship moving up the coast from Pukusa Point. Tracked him at 14 knots making us at first suspicious of his character, but as the range closed he was observed to be a large modern diesel freighter heavily loaded presenting a low silhouette. Moved on to his track and dived for one of those never failing crack-of-dawn attacks. Maneuvered for an 800 yard shot as he came by and fired three Mark 18 Mod. 1 bow torpedoes, spread to cover his length. The first two hit exactly as aimed sinking this overloaded ship immediately. Surfaced as soon as the smoke had cleared away to find no survivors and only wreckage and several empty landing craft half swamped, drifting about in the water. Proceeded at full power down the coast for a submerged patrol during the day well clear of the opposition which would arrive shortly. Dived off Pukusa Point where a north or south bound ship could be spotted coming in either direction, permitting a submerged attack if necessary, but preferably tracking until dark as these shallow waters cramped any ordinary evasion tactics. The west coast of Formosa is literally covered with airfields, and planes were in sight on practically every periscope observation.

1000 A strong northerly wind sprang up against the prevailing current which quickly whipped the surface into a sufficiently severe chop to make depth control difficult. This same chop, however, was soon to stand us in good stead for at noon the masts of another north bound freighter were sighted down the coast. He was running inside the 10 fathom curve zigging frequently. Though we could reach his track by moving in at high speed and have some battery left for evasion, our original plan of tracking till dark seemed more prudent under the circumstances. There then developed our longest submerged tracking problem in which we moved with our target 27 miles up the coast. This seem surprising but with the enemy zigging frequently and bucking a heavy wind and sea, his speed made good was little more than ours running on a straight course at 80 feet between observations. Our tracks converged and he passed directly over us at sundown.

Attack No. 2

At dark we surfaced 4,000 yards astern of him, passed him up at the same range, avoided a couple of stationary patrols, moved in to his track, then turned off for a stern shot as he came by. The night was black and spumey permitting us to lie with our stern to him at 800 yards as he bucked the heavy seas.

2100 With a salvo of three ready to fire with a liberal spread, fired a single Mark 18 Mod. 1 torpedo at his middle with practically zero gyro on a 76 port track. Our experience of the morning was not a mistake. We were clicking and this one hit with a terrific explosion. Only the first few members of the fire-control party to reach the bridge saw any of the ship before it went down. We now experienced something new in anti-submarine tactics in the nature of estimated 40 MM fire from the beach. It was directed straight up, however, and we were quite content to let them believe that our China based planes were aloft.

Proceeded down the coast avoiding the two stationary patrols and encountering a third which was quickly shaken off.

12 – 14 October 1944

0100 Sighted a properly lighted hospital ship on a northerly course which we looked over from close aboard. He appeared to be in every respect complying with International Law.

0800 Commenced submerged patrol off the Formosa coast. Only patrol boats and planes were sighted throughout the day. On surfacing proceeded to the northwest to a focal point of the probable shipping routes from both Takao and Kirun to Foochow. Foochow seemed the logical destination for any Japanese shipping in the Formosa ports which, forewarned, would be attempting to escape from our carrier strike. It turned out to be a focal point, but only for patrol craft. Much rainy, squally weather permitted getting clear of them on the surface after submerged approach, observation and evasion.

Conducted numerous searches along enemy retirement tracks until the Formosa strike was completed. On those which lead up close to Kirun the fires set by our boys were observed to be blazing furiously day and night.

15 – 17 October 1944

Moved over to the China coast and conducted submerged periscope patrol just south of Haitan Island. Only shipping of a thousand tons or less can follow the dangerous channels behind this island group. Our position appeared ideal to intercept any worthwhile shipping attempting to clear the Formosa area. However, absolutely nothing was sighted, so after two days in these treacherous waters we moved into the center of the Strait.

18 – 19 October 1944

Patrolled in Formosa Strait, encountering nothing but patrol craft. We were greeted on surfacing by radar-equipped planes who seemed to be assisted in their search by the patrols which also possessed radar. As it appeared to be more of a case of being hunted than hunting, we moved northeast to our original lucky spot off Pukusa Point, then on around the northern tip of the island to patrol off the port of Kirun. Friendly radar showed on our SJ to the east, probably one of the *Trigger – Silversides* group. Other radar continued to be so strong on our detector on all the usual frequencies that we stopped worrying about it except to fill in the necessary logs to help out in its future tabulation. Patrolling off Kirun was almost prohibitable due to the constantly changing weather and persistent large swells. The strong currents made it inadvisable to go very far into the outer harbor and the actual presence of shipping could not be determined.

19 October 1944

2230 Headed for the China Coast, having received word of an enemy task force heading north along the China Coast. Commenced a full power dash which would intercept them before dawn.

20 October 1944

0400 Made radar contact at 36,000 yards on an enemy group heading south instead of north as expected. There followed an approach which quickly developed into a trailing operation as our target, a *Katori* cruiser and two destroyers, were making 19 knots. Their erratic zigs at least every three minutes permitted us to close on the quarter where with a bit of luck or with stern torpedoes an attack would have been possible. Five times in a row we guessed wrong as to the direction of his next zig, and firing remained impossible as our slow Mark 18's just plain wouldn't make it before he would have been off on another leg.

As it was necessary to slow to twelve knots before releasing those torpedoes, and the cruiser would be opening the range during this slowing down period, it was necessary to reach a position not more than 600 yards astern of the cruiser for an up-the-tail shot. Dawn was approaching and so was the Formosa Bank just north of the Pescadoros, when we crawled into 800 yards. That is as far as we got, however, for he illuminated us. We got down before the bullets landed and expected a severe drubbing from depth charges. We were disappointed in the outcome, and swore never to be without steam torpedoes forward again.

The enemy evidently suspected other submarines and did not release the escort to work us over. A land-air and surface craft search started about dawn, but we were well to the north of their problem. On surfacing the hunt was still on and with a sick radar we went north clear of the Strait for repairs and a little rest from almost continuous operation.

21 October 1944

Continued submerged patrol north of the Formosa Strait then proceeded back to the China coast off Turnabout Island.

2000 Tracked and nearly fired on a PC-DE type patrol proceeding down the coast in dark stormy weather. We didn't like the looks of the situation as seas were rolling nearly over our bridge and his erractic zigs made a surface attack perilous. When the range was 2,000 yards with angle on the bow about 20°, as if by mutual consent the enemy reversed course and high tailed it. We did likewise, probably as happy as he was at the outcome. Our evasion course headed us back toward the Formosa coast so continued on for a submerged patrol on the following day.

22 October 1944

Continued on toward the coast commencing a submerged patrol at about 1000. The usual numerous aircraft were sighted during the day. Their quantity and types indicating an influx of planes probably as replenishments for those destroyed during the Formosa raids and very possibly also for support in the Philippines.

1800 Shortly after surfacing the SJ radar became temperamental and quit. Our industrious radar technician and officer commenced the usual non-stop repairs. Headed north for a safer operating area until they were completed, as this was no place to be operating without an SJ.

23 October 1944
Attack No. 3

 0030 On the first trial of the revamped SJ the operator reported land at 14,000 yards where no land should be. Commenced tracking, immediately discovering a small pip moving out in our direction. Put him astern and bent on the turns. He evidently lost his original contact on us for he changed course and commenced a wide swing about the convoy which was now also in sight. A submariner's dream quickly developed as we were able to assume the original position of this destroyer just ahead of the enemy while he went on a 2-mile inspection tour. The convoy was composed of three large modern tankers in column, a transport on the starboard beam, a freighter on the port beam, flanked by DE's on both beams and quarters. After zigging with the convoy in position 3,000 yards ahead we dropped back between the tankers and the freighter. On the next zig, stopped and turned right for nearly straight bow shots at the tankers as they came by, firing two torpedoes under the stack and engine room space of the nearest tanker, a single torpedo into the protruding stern of the middle tanker and two torpedoes under the stack and engine space of the far tanker. The minimum range was 300 yards and the maximum 800 yards. Torpedoes were exploding before the firing was completed and all hit as aimed. It was a terrific sight to see three blazing, sinking tankers but there was only time for just a glance, as the freighter was in position crossing our stern. Completed the set-up and was about to fire on this vessel when Leibold, my Boatswain's Mate, whom I've used for an extra set of eyes on all patrols, properly diagnosed the maneuver of the starboard transport who was coming in like a destroyer attempting to ram. We were boxed in by the sinking tankers, the transport was too close for us to dive, so we had to cross his bow. It was really a thriller-diller with the *Tang* barely getting on the inside of his turning circle and saving the stern with full left rudder in the last seconds. The transport commenced firing with large and small caliber stuff so cleared the bridge before realizing it was all above our heads. A quick glance aft, however, showed the tables were again turned for the transport was forced to continue her swing in an attempt to avoid colliding with the freighter which had also been coming in to ram. The freighter struck the transport's starboard quarter shortly after we commenced firing four stern torpedoes spread along their double length. At a range of 400 yards the crash coupled with the four torpedo explosions was terrific, sinking the freighter nose down almost instantly while the transport hung with a 30° up angle.

The destroyer was now coming in on our starboard quarter at 1,300 yards with DE's on our port bow and beam. We headed for the DE on our bow so as to get the destroyer astern and gratefully watched the DE turn away, he apparently having seen enough. Our destroyer still hadn't lighted off another boiler and it was possible to open the range slowly, avoiding the last interested DE. When the radar range to the DD was 4,500 yards he gave up the chase and returned to the scene of the transport. We moved back also, as his bow still showed on the radar and its pip was visible. When we were 6,000 yards off, however, another violent explosion took place and the bow disappeared both from sight and the radar screen. This explosion set off a gun duel amongst the destroyer and escort vessels who fired at random apparently sometimes at each other and sometimes just out into the night. Their confusion was truly complete. It looked like a good place to be away from so we cleared the area at full power until dawn.

Our attack log showed that only 10 minutes had elapsed from the time of firing our first torpedo until that final explosion when the transport's bow went under.

0600 Dived north of the Strait for submerged patrol.

2000 Surfaced. Nothing but patrol boats were sighted during the day, but at night a scene similar to the one previously encountered indicated the possibility of this being a trap. In any case there was little doubt about the heat being on in this area. Headed north where deeper water would at least give us a better sense of security.

24 October 1944

0600 Commenced submerged periscope patrol. On surfacing at dark looked for Turnabout Island feeling that all the Japs would now scarcely run traffic other than in the shallow protected water along the China coast. On approaching the islands at a range of 35,000 yards other than land pips [nothing] appeared on the radar screen until at tracking ranges the SJ was absolutely saturated.

The Staff had been correct in their estimate of the situation that the Japanese would likely send every available ship in support of the Philippine Campaign. The Leyte Campaign was in progress and the ships of this convoy as in the one of the 23rd were all heavily loaded. The tankers all carried planes on deck, and even the bows and sterns of the transports were piled high with apparent plane crates.

Attack No. 4

The convoy was tracked on courses following the rugged coast at 12 knots. The Japanese became suspicious during our initial approach, the escorts commencing to run an opposite course to the long column, firing bursts of 40 mm and 5" salvoes. As we continued to close the leading ships, the escort commander obligingly illuminated the column with 30" or 40" searchlight, using this to signal with. It gave us a perfect view of our first selected target, a three deck, two stack transport; of the second target, a three deck one stacker; and of the third, a large modern tanker. With ranges from 1,400 yards on the first transport to 500 yards on the tanker, fired two Mk. 18 torpedoes each in slow deliberate salvoes to pass under the foremast and mainmast of the first two vessels and under the middle and stern of the tanker. In spite of the apparent early warning and the sporadic shooting which was apparently designed to scare the submarine, no evasive tactics were employed by any of the ships. The torpedoes commenced hitting as we paralleled the convoy to search out our next two targets.

Our love for Mk. 18 Mod. 1 torpedoes after the disappointing cruiser experience was again restored as all torpedoes hit nicely. We passed the next ship, a medium freighter, abeam at 600 yards and then turned for a stern shot at another tanker and transport astern of her. Fired a single stern torpedo under the tanker's stack and one at the foremast and one at the mainmast of the transport. The ranges were between 600 and 700 yards. Things were anything but calm and peaceful now, for the escorts had stopped their warning tactics and were directing good salvoes at us and the blotches of smoke we left behind on going to full power to pull clear of the melee. Just after firing on the transport, a full fledged destroyer charged under her stern and headed our way. What exactly next took place in the following seconds will never be determined, but the tanker was hit nicely and blew up, apparently a gasoline loaded job. At least one torpedo was observed to hit the transport and an instant later the destroyer blew up, either intercepting our third torpedo or possibly the 40 mm fire from the DE's bearing down on our beam. In any case, the result was the same and only the transport remained afloat and she apparenty stopped.

We were as yet untouched, all gunfire either having cleared over our heads or being directed at the several blurps of smoke we emitted when pleading for more speed. When 10,000 yards from the transport we were all in the clear so stopped to look over the situation and re-check our last two torpedoes which had both been loaded forward during our stern tube attack.

A half hour was spent with each torpedo, withdrawing it from the tube, ventilating the battery and checking the rudders and gyros. With everything in readiness started cautiously back in to get our cripple. The two DE's were patrolling on his seaward side, so made a wide sweep and came in very slow so as not to be detected even by sound. She was lower in the water but not definitely sinking. Checking our speed by pit log at 6 knots, fired our 23rd torpedo from

900 yards, aimed just forward of her mainmast. Observed the phosphorescent wake heading as aimed at our crippled target, fired our 24th and last torpedo at his foremast. Rang up emergency speed as this last torpedo broached and curved sharply to the left. Completed part of a fishtail maneuver in a futile attempt to clear the turning circle of the erratic circular run. The torpedo was observed throughout 100% of its turn due to the phosphorescence of its wake. It struck abreast the after torpedo room with a violent explosion about 20 seconds after firing. The tops were blown off the only regular ballast tanks aft and the after three compartments flooded instantly. The *Tang* sank by the stern much as you would drop a pendulum suspended in a horizontal position. There was insufficient time even to carry out the last order to close the hatch. One consolation for those of us washed off into the water was the explosion of our 23rd torpedo and observation of our last target settling by the stern. Those who escaped in the morning were greeted by the transport's bow sticking straight out of the water a thousand yards or so away.

(C) WEATHER

Normal for locality patrol.

(D) TIDAL INFORMATION

Normal.

(E) NAVIGATIONAL AIDS

As listed in navigational aids.

(F) SHIP CONTACTS

See narrative.

(G) AIRCRAFT CONTACTS

See narrative.

(H) ATTACK DATA

See attached report forms.

U.S.S. *Tang*   Torpedo Attack No. 1   Patrol No. 5
Time: Dawn   Date: 11 October 1944   Position: North of Pakusa
                                            Point, Formosa

TARGET DATA – DAMAGE INFLICTED

Description	Single Unescorted large modern diesel driven freighter proceeding northward from Pakusa Point, Formosa, at 14 knots. Ship was heavily loaded and presented a low silhouette. Original contact was by radar at 17,000 yards followed by good visual observation. Firing range was 800 yards.
Ship(s) Sunk	1 large freighter (EU) – 7,500 tons.
Ship(s) Damaged or Probably Sunk	None
Damage Determined by	Observed two torpedo hits out of three fired from range of 800 yards. Observed ship blow up and sink almost immediately after two torpedoes hit. Surfaced and searched wreckage, but found no survivors.
Target Data } Own Ship Data }	Not available due to loss of records in *Tang*.

FIRE CONTROL AND TORPEDO DATA

Type Attack	Target tracked on surface to determine speed. Dove just before dawn on targets tracked for submerged attack. Fired 3 Mark 18 Mod. 1 torpedoes from bow tubes spread to cover length of target. Two hits were observed exactly as shown.

NOTE: Torpedo data not available due to loss of records in *Tang*.

U.S.S. *Tang*   Torpedo Attack No. 2   Patrol No. 5
Time: 2100 Item   Date: 11 October 1944   Position: North of Pakusa Point

TARGET DATA – DAMAGE INFLICTED

Description: Single north bound unescorted freighter similar
                            to *Aden Maru* Class (5,324 tons). Freighter picked
                            up by periscope at 1,000 yards tracked until dawn.
                            Heavy air activity prevented surfacing. Heavy
                            seas and fresh wind with radical zigs of target
                            permitted tracking of this target until darkness.
                            Ship passed directly overhead at dusk. After
                            dark surfaced 4,000 yards astern of target avoided
                            2 stationary patrols to gain position ahead for
                            stern tube attack.

Ships sunk   1 Freighter similar to *Aden Maru* Class (EC)
                            (5,324 tons)

Ship(s) Damaged or
Probably Sunk   None

Damage Determined   Observed ship blow up and sink following single
by   torpedo hit fired from range of 500 yards.

Target Data   }   Not available due to loss of records in *Tang*.
Own Ship Data }

FIRE CONTROL AND TORPEDO DATA

Type Attack   Night surface attack. Fired single Mark 18 Mod 1
                            torpedo from stern tube at range of 500 yards on
                            75° port track. Torpedo hit amidships. Speed
                            had been previously determined by tracking sub-
                            merged for eleven hours.

NOTE: Torpedo data not available due to loss or records in *Tang*.

U.S.S. *Tang*   Torpedo Attack No. 3   Patrol No. 5
Time: Early Morning   Date: 23 October 1944   Position: NW of Formosa

TARGET DATA – DAMAGE INFLICTED

Description	Convoy contacted by radar consisting of three large tankers in column with a medium transport to starboard (west) and a large freighter to port (east). Escorted by a destroyer steaming ahead of formation and DEs on each beam and quarter. Leading DD gained contact, but lost initial contact. *Tang* took position 3,000 yards ahead of convoy to check speed and then dropped back between tankers and freighters. Following a zig turned right for nearly straight bow shots on tankers. After firing 2 torpedoes at leading tanker, 1 at overlapping middle tanker and 2 at trailing tanker, *Tang* barely escaped being rammed by transport. The transport continued to swing and was struck on starboard quarter by the freighter who also was attempting to ram. Four torpedoes were fired at these two ships. The collision and hitting of torpedoes occurred about simultaneously. Tang evaded escorts on the surface after being subjected to heavy but inaccurate gun fire from transport and escorts.

Ship(s) Sunk	1 large tanker (EU)	–	10,000 tons
	1 large tanker (EU)	–	10,000 tons
	1 large tanker (EU)	–	10,000 tons
	1 Medium transport (EU)	–	7,500 tons
	1 large freighter (EU)	–	7,500 tons

Ship(s) Damaged or Probably Sunk	None

Damage Determined by	Observed two hits in leading tanker, one in middle tanker and two in trailing tanker. All were observed to burn fiercely and sink. The transport was rammed on the starboard quarter

by the freighter. Four torpedoes were fired at overlapping freighter and transport. Freighter sank almost immediately bows first. Transport settled by the stern. Ten minutes later a violent explosion occurred and transport's bow disappeared from view and radar screen.

Target Data   }
Own Ship Data }   Not available due to loss of records in *Tang*.

FIRE CONTROL AND TORPEDO DATA

Type Attack   Night surface attack using radar ranges and TBT bearings. Ranges on firing at the three tankers varied from 300 to 800 yards. Range on firing at the combined transport and freighter was 400 yards.

NOTE: Torpedo data not available due to loss of records in *Tang*.

U.S.S. *Tang*   Torpedo Attack No. 4   Patrol No. 5
Time: Early Evening Date: 24 October 1944   Position: China Coasts between
Foochow and Amoy

TARGET DATA – DAMAGE INFLICTED

Description:

Contact was by radar in early evening on convoy
of large ships proceeding South, hugging the
coast, at 12 knots. Convoy consisted of at
least 14 large vessels in column escorted by
at least 1 fleet type DD and twelve DEs. Some
of the DEs initially were to seaward of the
convoy while the DD and other DEs were on the
landward side.

During the initial approach presence of *Tang*
was apparently suspected as seaward DEs commenced firing at random. Approach was continued on leading vessels as a large searchlight
was trained down the column illuminating a 3
deck 2 stack transport, a 3 deck single stack
transport and a large modern tanker.

Two torpedoes each were fired to hit these
three vessels as convoy took avoiding action.
Tang then took parallel opposite course to remaining ships, passed up a medium freighter at
600 yards to fire one torpedo at a large tanker
and two at a large transport while escorts
fired at *Tang* and her engine smoke.

A fleet type destroyer came around the stern
of the transport as firing was completed, but
either hit a *Tang* torpedo or ran into cross
fire on the escorts as she blew up.

Tang pulled clear to check the last two torpedoes while the situation cleared.

Returning to the last transport fired last two
torpedoes to finish her off.

Ship(s) Sunk			
1 large AP (EU)	–	10,000 tons
1 large AP (EU)	–	10,000 tons
1 medium AP (EU)	–	7,500 tons

1 large AO (EU)	–	10,000 tons
1 large AO (EU)	–	10,000 tons
1 Fleet type DD (EU)	–	1,500 tons

Ship(s) Damaged or Probably Sunk

None

Damage Determined by

All torpedoes were observed to hit and all ships seen to sink, the second tanker and the DD blowing up completely. The bow of the last last transport was observed by *Tang* survivors the next morning sticking straight up out of the water.

Target Data }
Own Ship Data }

Not available due to loss of records in *Tang*.

FIRE CONTROL AND TORPEDO DATA

Type Attack

This was a night surface attack using radar ranges and TBT bearings. The bow tubes were split, two each, to hit the three leading ships at ranges varying from 1,400 yards down to 900 yards.

Passing up the next ship in column, a medium freighter, fired a single torpedo to hit a large tanker and two more to hit a transport at ranges between six and seven hundred yards.

Returning to the scene, after checking the last two torpedoes, fired two single shots at the stopped sinking transport.

NOTE: Torpedo data not available due to loss of records in *Tang*.

(R) MILES STEAM – FUEL USED

Not available due to loss of records in *Tang*.

(S) DURATION

Days enroute to area	15
Days in area	14
Days enroute to base	—
Days submerged	10

(T) FACTORS OF ENDURANCE REMAINING

Torpedoes	Fuel Gals.	Provisions Days	Personnel Factor Days
0	—	—	—

(U) COMMUNICATIONS, RADAR AND SONAR COUNTERMEASURES

Not availabe due to loss of records in *Tang*.

(V) REMARKS

Report on the Loss of the U.S.S. *Tang* (SS306)

Introduction

This report is compiled from my observation and the stories of the eight other survivors as related to me at the first opportunity after capture.

The U.S.S. *Tang* took on board the twenty-four Mark 18 Mod 1 electric torpedoes prepared for the U.S.S. *Tambor* who was being delayed. All torpedo personnel in the *Tang* had attended electric torpedo school and it is assured those torpedoes were properly routined while on station. In fact, the performance of the first twenty-three torpedoes in all running perfectly, with twenty-two hits, attests to this.

The last two torpedoes were loaded in tubes three and four during the final stern tube attack. After pulling clear of the enemy escorts opportunity was available to spend an hour checking these torpedoes before closing the enemy to sink the cripple. They were partially withdrawn from the tubes, batteries ventilated, gyro pots inspected and steering mechanism observed to be operating freely.

With the submarine speed checking at six knots and the ship conned for zero gyro, the twenty-third torpedo was fired. When its phosphorescent wake was observed heading for its point of aim on the stopped transport, the last torpedo was fired from tube number four. This torpedo curved sharply to the left, broaching during the first part of its turn and then porpoising during remainder. Emergency speed was called for and answered immediately on firing, and a fishtail maneuver partially completed in an attempt to get clear of the torpedo's turning circle. This resulted only in the torpedo striking the stern abreast the after torpedo room instead of amidships.

The explosion was very violent, whipping the boat, breaking H.P. air lines, lifting deck plates, etc. Numerous personnel as far forward as the control room received broken limbs and other injuries. The immediate result to the ship was to flood the after three compartments together with number six and seven ballast tanks. No one escaped from these compartments and even the forward engine room was half flooded before the after door could be secured.

The ship, with no normal positive buoyancy aft and with three after flooded compartments, went down instantly by the stern. With personnel in the conning tower and on the bridge falling aft due to the angle, there was insufficient time to to carry out the order to close the hatch.

Personnel in the control room succeeded in closing the conning tower lower hatch, but it had been jimmied in the explosion and leaked badly. They then leveled the boat off by flooding number two main ballast tank (opening the vents only) and proceeded to the forward torpedo room carrying the injured in blankets.

When the survivors from the forward engine room and after battery compartments reached the mess room, they found water already above the eye-port in the door to the control room. On closing the bulkhead flappers in the ventilation piping they found the water not yet at this height. They therefore, opened the door, letting the water race through, then proceeded on to the torpedo room. This made a total of about thirty men to reach the escape position.

During this time all secret and confidential publications were destroyed first by burning in the control room, and then in the forward battery compartment as the control room flooded. This latter seems unfortunate since a great deal of the smoke entered the forward torpedo room.

Escaping was delayed by the presence of Japanese patrols which ran close by dropping occasional depth charges. This is unfortunate for an electrical fire in the forward battery was becoming severe. Commencing at about six o'clock, four parties left the ship, but only with difficultly as the pressure at one hundred and eighty feet made numerous returns to the torpedo room necessary to revive prostrate men.

At the time the last party escaped, the forward battery fire had reached such intensity that paint on the forward torpedo room after bulkhead was scorched and running down. Considerable pressure had built up in the forward battery making it difficult to secure the after torpedo room door sufficiently tight to prevent acrid smoke from seeping by the gasket. It is felt that this gasket blew out, either due to the pressure or an ensuing battery explosion, and that the remaining personnel were asphixiated.

Of the thirteen men who escaped, five were able to cling to the buoy until picked up. Three others reached the surface, but were unable to hang on or breathe and floated off and drowned. The other five were not seen after leaving the trunk.

Of the nine officers and men on the bridge, three were able to swim throughout the night and until picked up eight hours later. One officer escaped from the flooded conning tower and remained afloat until rescued with the aid of his trousers converted to a life belt[2].

The Destroyer Escort[3] which picked up all nine survivors was one of the four which were rescuing Japanese troops and personnel. When we realized that our clubbings and kickings were being administered by the burned, mutilated survivors of our own handiwork, we found we could take it with less prejudice.

---

[2]   Lieutenant Larry Savadkin.
[3]   IJN *P-34.*

FF12-10(A)/A16-3(18) Submarine Force, Pacific Fleet

bn

Serial 02379 Care of Fleet Post Office,

San Francisco, California,

<u>CLASSIFIED</u> 25 Sept. 1945

<u>First Endorsement to</u> Note: This report will be

Tang Report of destroyed prior to

Fifth War Patrol. entering patrol area.

ComSubPac Patrol Report No. <u>928</u>
U.S.S. *Tang* – Fifth War Patrol

From: The Commander Submarine Force, Pacific Fleet.
To: The Commander in Chief, United States Fleet.
Via: The Commander in Chief, U.S. Pacific Fleet.

Subject: U.S.S. *Tang* (SS306) – Report of Fifth War Patrol
(24 September to 25 October 1944).

1. The fifth war patrol of the U.S.S. *Tang*, commanded by Commander R. H. O'Kane, U.S. Navy, was conducted in the Formosa Strait. This report, written from memory after Commander O'Kane's release from a Japanese prisoner of war camp, is not as complete or detailed as is customary nor is it feasible to obtain division and squadron commanders endorsement of it.

2. The Force Commander considers the fifth patrol of the *Tang* to be one of the great submarine cruises of all time. The fight was relentlessly carried to the enemy throughout, and in four precisely executed attacks a total of thirteen enemy ships were destroyed. The first two were unopposed attacks against single ships, but the last two were stirring actions of *Tang*, unsupported, against large, well armed and heavily escorted convoys. Data is not available on which to base an analysis of these attacks, however the necessity for analysis diminishes when it is realized that twenty-two of the twenty-four torpedoes fired hit, and one of the remaining two is known to have run erratic. This performance, especially under the strain of such lively action as attacks three and four, eloquently bespeaks firm and competent command, perfectly organized and thoroughly drilled fire control and ship control parties and meticulous attention to the details of preservation and maintenance.

3. The award of the Submarine Combat Insignia for this patrol is authorized.

4.   It was the tragic result of one of the unavoidable risks of submarine warfare that this gallant ship should be sunk by the malfunctioning of one of her own torpedoes, and that the last to be fired. To those who survived the Commander Submarine Force, Pacific Fleet, extends a heartfelt welcome and his sympathy on the loss of their shipmates. To the *Tang* and to the courageous men who manned her he offers his admiring congratulations on a brilliant patrol during which the following damage was inflicted on the enemy:

SUNK

1 – AK (EU)	–	7,500 tons	(Torpedo Attack No. 1)
1 – AK (*Aden Maru* Class) (EC)	–	5,824 tons	(Torpedo Attack No. 2)
3 – AO, Large (EU)	–	30,000 tons	(Torpedo Attack No. 3)
1 – AP, Medium (EU)	–	7,500 tons	(Torpedo Attack No. 3)
1 – AK, Large (EU)	–	7,500 tons	(Torpedo Attack No. 3)
2 – AP, Large (EU)	–	20,000 tons	(Torpedo Attack No. 4)
1 – AP, Medium (EU)	–	7,500 tons	(Torpedo Attack No. 4)
2 – AO, Large (EU)	–	20,000 tons	(Torpedo Attack No. 4)
1 – DD (EU	–	1,500 tons	(Torpedo Attack No. 4)
TOTAL SUNK		107,824 tons	

G.C. Crawford
Chief of Staff

Distribution:
(Complete Reports)

Cominch	(7)	Comsubspac	(3)
CNO	(5)	ComsubspacAdCond	(40)
Cincpac	(6)	SUBAD, MI	(2)
JICPOA	(1)	ComsubspaceSubordcom	(3)
Comservpac	(1)	All Squadron and Div.	
Cinclant	(1)	Commanders, Pacific	(2)
Comsubslant	(8)	ComSubOpTrnSr	(3)
S/N School, NL	(2)	Substrainpac	(2)
CO, S/M Base, PH	(1)	All Submarines,	
Comsopac	(2)	Pacific	(1)
Comsowespac	(1)		
Comsubs7thFlt (Fwd Echolon)	(2)	E.L. Hymes, 2nd,	
Comsubs7thFlt (Rear Echelon)	(2)	Flag Secretary.	
Comnorpac	(1)		

Appendix I
U.S.S. Tang, Sailing List, Patrol 5

Accardy, John G.	SM3	
Adams, Ralph F.	StM2	
Allen, Dwayne D.	MoMM2	
Anderson, Philip E.	TM3	
Andriolo, CharlesL	RM2	
Anthony, Homer	F1	
Beaumont, E.H.	LT	
Bergman, Edwin F.	RM1	
Bisogno, Frederick N	TM3	
Boucher, Wilfred J	TM3	
Bresette, Bernard	S1	
Bush, John	EM2	
Caverly, Floyd M.	RT1	(Survivor)
Chiavetta, Benjamin	S1	
Clark, Walter J.	S1	
Coffin, Robert J	EM3	
Culp, James H.	CEM	
Da Silva, Jesse B.	MoMM3	(Survivor)
Darienzo, Arthur J.	EM2	
De Lapp, Marvin V.	CMoMM	
Decker, Clayton O.	MoMM3	(Survivor)
Dorsey, William E.	MoMM1	
Enos, F.M., Jr.	LT(jg)	
Erickson, Lawrence H.	F1	
Fellicetty, Daniel C.	Y3	

Finckbone, Bruce H.	EM2	
Flanagan, Henry J.	Lt(jg)	(Survivor)
Fluker, John W.	TM1	
Foster, John M.	TM1	
Galloway, William C.	TM2	
Gentle, Thomas E.	F1	
Gorab, George J., Jr.	EM3	
Gregg, Osmer D.	S1	
Hainline, Howard W.	S1	
Harms, Frank G.	MoMM2	
Haws, Glen O.	MoMM3	
Henry, John F.	F1	
Heubeck, J.H.	LT(jg)	
Hudson, Albert L	CMoMM	
Ijames, Homer W., Jr.	S2	
Imwald, Stewart S.	MoMM2	
Jenkins, Donald M.	S1	
Jones, Sidney W.	CQM	
Kaiser, Louis C.	MoMM3	
Kanagy, John T.	EM1	
Kassube, John T.	S1	
Key, John A.	SC3	
Knapp, Ralph B.	FC3	
Kroth, Richard J.	LT(jg)	
Lane, Le Roy R.	EM1	
Larson, Paul L.	CPhM	
Lee, Robert P.	RM3	
Leibold, William R.	CBM	(Survivor)
Llewellyn, Lindley H.	RM3	
London, Charles W.	F1	
Loveless, Chester	EM1	
Lytton, Ellroy	MoMM1	
McMorrow, Robert V.	MoMM2	
McNabb, John J.	F1	
Narowanski, Pete	TM3	(Survivor)
O'Kane, Richard H.	CDR – CO	(Survivor)
Parker, John J.	CCS	
Pearce, B.C., Jr.	ENS	
Raiford, Rubin M.	Ck3	
Reabuck, F.J.	F1	

Rector, Darrell D.	GM3	
Reinhardt, Ernest	F1	
Roberts, James D.	SC3	
Robertson, George L.	MoMM2	
Savadkin, L.	LT	(Survivor)
Smith, Seymour G., Jr.	QM3	
Springer, F.H.	LT – XO	
Stepien, Edward F.	F1	
Sunday, Fred L.	EM3	
Trukke, Hayes O.	TM2	(Survivor)
Vaughn, Paul B., Jr.	Cox	
Wadsworth, Charles W.	TM3	
Walker, Howard M.	StM1	
Weekley, Leland S.	CTM	
Welch, Robert E.	QM3	
White, James M.	GM1	
Williams, Walter H.	Y2	
Wines, P.T.	LT (jg)	
Wukovich, George	MoMM1	
Zofcin, George	MoMM1	

Appendix II
Allied Code Names for Japanese Aircraft

Name	Manufacturer & Model	Type
Belle	Kawanishi H3K1	Flying boat
Betty	Mitsubishi G6M1	Twin-engine bomber
Cherry	Kugisho H5Y	Flying boat
Claude	Mitsubishi A5M	Carrier based fighter
Dave	Nakajima E8N1	Reconnaissance seaplane
Dinah	Mitsubishi Ki-46	Reconnaissance plane
Emily	Kawanishi H8K	Flying boat
Glen	Kugisho E14Y1	Small reconnaissance seaplane
Hank	Aichi E10A1	Reconnaissance seaplane
Jake	Aichi E13A1	Reconnaissance seaplane
Jean	Kugisho B4Y1	Carrier based attack bomber
Kate	Nakajima B5N1 & 2	Carrier based attack bomber
Laura	Aichi E11A1	Reconnaissance seaplane
Lily	Kawasaki Ki-48	Twin-engine bomber
Mavis	Kawanishi H6K	Type 97 flying boat
Nell	Mitsubishi G3M	Attack bomber
Nick	Kawasaki Ki-45	Two-seat fighter
Norm	Kawanishi E15K1	Reconnaissance seaplane
Oscar	Nakajima Ki-43	Fighter
Pete	Mitsubishi F1M1	Observation seaplane
Rufe	Nakajima A6M2-N	Float plane version of Zero fighter
Sally	Mitsubishi Ki-21	Heavy bomber
Val	Aichi D3A	Carrier based bomber
Zeke	Mitsubishi A6M	Carrier based fighter, Zero

Appendix III
Ship Type Designations

The United States Navy used letter codes to designate various ship types. In Navy use, these were prefixed to the ship's hull number. Submarines used the same codes to identify target types, applying the military type designation to both actual naval vessels and to civilian ships of the same general type.

AD	Destroyer Tender
AK	Freighter
AM	Minesweeper
AO	Fleet Oiler; Tanker
AP	Transport
AS	Submarine Tender
ASR	Submarine Rescue Vessel
AV	Seaplane Tender
BB	Battleship
CA	Heavy Cruiser
CL	Light Cruiser
CV	Aircraft Carrier
CVE	Escort Aircraft Carrier
CVL	Light Aircraft Carrier
DD	Destroyer
DE	Destroyer Escort
DMS	Destroyer Minesweeper
PC	Patrol Craft
PCE	Patrol Craft, Escort
PT	PT Boat
PY	Patrol Yacht
SC	Sub Chaser
SS	Submarine

Appendix IV
The Mark 18 Torpedo

In his book about his experiences in *Tang*, Rear Admiral Richard H. O'Kane commented on the frequent torpedo shortages inflicting the submarine service in the Pacific. When it came to shortages involving *Tang*, one might be forgiven for suggesting that they were partly O'Kane's fault. He proved to be such an outstanding ship hunter that *Tang*'s four anti-shipping patrols averaged only 35½ days and ended when *Tang* ran out of torpedoes. Her second patrol, which was almost entirely taken up by lifeguard duty and did not include any attacks on enemy shipping, lasted 61 days, which was closer to the average for most boats.

The shortages affected the torpedoes *Tang* carried on her fifth and final war patrol. These had been intended for loading aboard *Tambor* (SS-198), but the much older submarine had been delayed and *Tang* received them instead. The entire load of 24 torpedoes consisted of Mark 18 Mod. 1 electric types. O'Kane suggested in his book that this, in itself, spoke to shortages, for the usual practice was to supply a boat with a mixed load of electric and steam torpedoes.

During his pursuit of the *Katori* class cruiser on *Tang*'s fifth patrol, O'Kane indicated that this brought home the need for steam torpedoes in the bow tubes. The slower speed of the electric types had necessitated closing to too short a range during a stern chase, resulting in a missed opportunity for a shot at the cruiser. He clearly felt that the faster steam torpedoes (46 knots vs. 29 knots for the Mark 18) would have allowed him to make an attack.

When equipped with steam torpedoes, *Tang* carried Mark 14 and Mark 23 models. These were identical, except that the Mark 23 did not have the 31-knot low-speed setting of the Mark 14. This was rarely used in any case, though after the war the Mark 23 was eliminated while the Mark 14, considered more versatile, continued in service until the 1970s. On at least one occasion, O'Kane mentions firing a Mark 14 in the patrol report narrative, but the torpedo data in the attack report shows that this was actually a Mark 23.

The one thing that could be said for the Mark 14 was that, once initial problems were fixed, it was reliable. That it required nearly 20 months before it attaining this reliability must serve as an indictment of the Navy's Bureau of Ordnance, which brushed aside complaints of unreliability and blamed the captains for sloppy marksmanship. It could equally be considered an indictment of a parsimonious Congress, which never gave the Navy enough money to conduct proper torpedo tests before the war.

Torpedoes were expensive, and so were the old ships that would have to be used as targets in proper tests. Consequently, BuOrd settled for testing torpedoes with exercise heads or relying on engineering studies, both of which seemed to indicate there would be no problem in the field. So when the reports came in that the Mark 14 was running too deep, and that the magnetic feature on its Mark 6 exploder frequently either failed to detonate at all, or set off the warhead prematurely, BuOrd shrugged off the possibility that there was anything wrong with the design and blamed the captains.

Ultimately, field tests proved conclusively that the Mark 14 torpedo ran an average of 11 feet deeper than set, and that both the magnetic and contact features of the Mark 6 exploder were unreliable. The magnetic feature never did work correctly, and was ordered deactivated. The contact exploder was initially fixed at the Pearl Harbor Torpedo Shop, after experiments isolated the problem, with BuOrd, reluctantly, providing a permanent fix once confronted with irrefutable evidence.

The Mark 14 had one primary disadvantage. The wet heater (steam) propulsion system's exhaust left a clearly noticeable wake. Alert lookouts were sometimes able to spot the wake of an approaching torpedo, allowing the target to avoid the torpedo. Worse, following the wakes back to their source gave enemy anti-submarine units a starting place for their counterattacks. What was needed was a wakeless torpedo.

The solution was the Mark 18 electric torpedo. While BuOrd had been working on their own electric torpedo, the Mark 18 was a product of private industry. Westinghouse took a captured German G7e electric torpedo and built a version that would work in American torpedo tubes.

In his book, O'Kane was not kind to Westinghouse and the other contractors who provided the control mechanism for the Mark 18. Erratic operation, including broaching or running in a circle, was an occasional problem with all torpedo models, but the Mark 18s seemed particular prone to this sort of thing.

In his own book, *Salt & Steel: Reflections of a Submariner,* Edward L. Beach speculated that as many as ten of our submarines may have been sunk by their own torpedoes. Two, *Tang* and *Tullibee* (SS-284) were definitely lost to this cause, as their survivors reported after the war. Beach suggested that, given this number of known losses, it would be a reasonable statistical probability that another eight of the 28 boats lost to unknown causes may also have been victims of their own torpedoes.

The United States was not alone in having torpedo problems. The Germans experienced the same problems with depth keeping, unreliable magnetic exploders, and defective contact exploders. The Germans, however, proved a bit more amenable to listening to their captains when they reported the problems, so they were fixed somewhat faster.

Japan, which had done extensive pre-war torpedo testing, never experienced these problems in combat. The failures of the Japanese submarine service to exert a decisive effect on the war was due more to doctrinal failures than defective equipment. Their torpedoes generally had a longer range, bigger warheads, and greater reliability than our own. Negating this, their high command consistently misused their submarines in support of a flawed fleet doctrine, rather than sending them on the anti-commerce missions which proved so effective for German and American boats.

Printed in the United States
114329LV00004B/192/A

9 781932 606058